SOCIAL DEFENCE
SOCIAL CHANGE

By the same Author

The Bias of Science (1979)

Changing the Cogs: Activists and the Politics of Technology (1979)

Nuclear Knights (1980)

Uprooting War (1984)*

Intellectual Suppression: Australian Case Histories, Analysis and Responses
(co-editor) (1986)

Scientific Knowledge in Controversy: The Social Dynamics of the Fluoridation Debate (1991)

Strip the Experts (1991)*

*Freedom Press titles

SOCIAL DEFENCE
SOCIAL CHANGE
by
Brian Martin

FREEDOM PRESS
London
1993

First published
1993
by FREEDOM PRESS
84B Whitechapel High St
London E1 7QX

© Brian Martin & Freedom Press

ISBN 0 900384 69 7

Typeset by Brian Martin
Printed in Gt Britain by Aldgate Press, London E1 7QX

Contents

1 Introduction *1*
2 Some basics *4*
3 Elite reform or grassroots initiative? *27*
4 Steven Huxley and "nonviolent" struggle *38*
5 Lessons from the Fiji coups *50*
6 Nonviolence against hypocrisy in the Gulf *66*
7 Revolutionary social defence *69*
8 A tool for feminists? *80*
9 What about the police? *89*
10 Social defence and the environment *96*
11 Science and technology for nonviolent struggle *106*
12 Telecommunications for nonviolent struggle *111*
13 Towards a resilient political system *120*
14 Towards a resilient economic system *132*
15 Postscript: Power tends to corrupt, even social defence *141*
    Further reading *145*
    Index *148*

Publishers' Note

In our opinion Brian Martin's book is an important contribution to the idea of social defence, that is, to quote his own words: "of abolishing military forces and relying in their stead on non-violent struggles by the general population".

We are sure there will be many anarchists who agree with his approach. Many more would agree with all his conclusions if they were clear in their minds as to how Brian Martin imagines that the military forces will be "abolished" in the first place. The "non-violent" and the so-called "violent" anarchists have been debating for a very long time not only how to get rid of the military, but also of privilege. The columns of *Freedom* are witness to this fact!

By sheer coincidence FREEDOM PRESS are publishing a small volume *Violence and Anarchism* – a polemic – made up of editorials and Readers' responses from *Freedom* in 1960 sparked off by an Editorial which lamented the fact that an *attentat* by a white farmer, David Pratt, on the South African dictator Dr. Verwoerd, an outstanding advocate of apartheid, had only wounded him.

We feel both volumes should be read by "activists" if the magnitude of the problem facing all those of us who actively seek to advance to a truly non-violent world, is to be fully appreciated.

Acknowledgements

This book would have never been possible without the support, encouragement and insight of many activists and scholars over the years, especially members of Schweik Action Wollongong and Canberra Peacemakers and many correspondents from around the world. I thank Robert Burrowes, Felice and Jack Cohen-Joppa, Steve Huxley, Denis Pym, Christine Schweitzer, Miriam Solomon, Ralph Summy, Wendy Varney and John Zube for helpful comments on earlier drafts of the text. John Zube's comments were so extensive that it was impossible to do justice to them. Those who would like to learn about his vision of "panarchy" can reach him at 7 Oxley Street, Berrima NSW 2577, Australia.

Parts of this book have been adapted from previous writings: "Social defence: arguments and actions," in Brian Martin et al., *Nonviolent Struggle and Social Defence*, edited by Shelley Anderson and Janet Larmore (London: War Resisters' International, 1991), pp. 81-141 (chapter 2); "Social defence: elite reform or grassroots initiative?" *Social Alternatives*, vol. 6, no. 2, April 1987, pp. 19-23 (chapter 3); "Learning about 'nonviolent' struggle: lessons from Steven Huxley," *Nonviolence Today*, #22, August-September 1991, pp. 11-14 (chapter 4); "Lessons in nonviolence from the Fiji coups," *Gandhi Marg*, vol. 10, no. 6, September 1988, pp. 326-339 (chapter 5); "Resist repressive regimes," leaflet by Schweik Action Wollongong, 1987 (table on social offence in chapter 5); "Gulf War shows it's time to set our own agenda," *Peace News*, July 1991, p. 2 (chapter 6); "Revolutionary social defence," *Bulletin of Peace Proposals*, vol. 22, no. 1, March 1991, pp. 97-105 (chapter 7); "Science for non-violent struggle," *Science and Public Policy*, vol. 19, no. 1, February 1992, pp. 55-58 (chapter 11); Schweik Action Wollongong, "Telecommunications for nonviolent struggle," *Civilian-Based Defense: News & Opinion*, vol. 7, no. 6, August 1992, pp. 7-10 (chapter 12). In each case I've revised the material. Referencing has been kept to a minimum.

I would be pleased to correspond with anyone concerning matters covered in this book. Contact me at: Department of Science and Technology Studies, University of Wollongong, Wollongong NSW 2522, Australia; e-mail: B.Martin@uow.edu.au.

FREEDOM PRESS publishes *Freedom* fortnightly, *The Raven* quarterly, and anarchist books and pamphlets (currently sixty five titles in print).

Freedom is a propaganda newspaper, commenting on world affairs from an anarchist point of view. The first edition appeared in October 1886. Its style has always been discursive, seeking to disseminate anarchism by getting anarchist ideas discussed by readers outside the anarchist movement.

The Raven is a quarterly magazine of 96 pages, dealing with anarchist ideas at greater length. Recent issues have included collections of essays on Education, Revolution, Communication and Health.

FREEDOM PRESS has published books and pamphlets for more than a century. These include classic and recent statements of the anarchist case, history books, hilarious cartoon books, and anarchist treatments of particular aspects of life. The Anarchist Discussion series was begun in 1991.

Freedom Press Bookshop, open six days a week, also sells works of anarchist interest from commercial and academic publishers, across the counter and by mail order. The shop entrance is in Angel Alley, a long passage approached by a pedestrian tunnel, alongside the Whitechapel Art Gallery.

Send for a free specimen copy of *Freedom* and a list of over 400 titles, many of them post free.

FREEDOM PRESS
84b Whitechapel High Street, London E1 7QX.

1
Introduction

The idea of social defence—namely of abolishing military forces and relying in their stead on nonviolent struggles by the general population—is extremely radical. Yet a large amount of the writing on this subject is set within the most conservative of assumptions about society. It is assumed that it is somehow possible to introduce social defence and yet leave much of society the same: the same economic system, the same political structures, the same scientific and health systems, and so on.

To me this is implausible. The military is one of the keys to protecting existing systems of power. Remove the military and the scope for change would be greatly increased. Furthermore, training people in methods of nonviolent struggle against outside aggressors would also give them the skills to challenge employers, politicians, sexual exploiters and many others.

Many nonviolent activists are well aware of the connection between nonviolent action and social change. That is exactly why they are responsive to the idea of social defence.

By contrast, though, some of the most prominent writers on social defence—such as Gene Sharp, Adam Roberts and Theodor Ebert—take a position that downplays social change. They focus on defending the state and the existing society. They see social defence as a logical option to be implemented by governments.

My disagreement with these scholars is a friendly one. They have contributed enormously to increasing knowledge about nonviolent struggle and to public awareness of social defence. Indeed, it is precisely because their contributions are so important that their assumptions should be scrutinised and alternatives considered.

This book is a contribution to that process. I have tried to spell out some of the radical implications and connections that flow from the idea of social defence. Inevitably some of this is speculative. People's experiences with nonviolent struggle are necessary to test and to reject or refine ideas about social defence.

In chapters 2-7, I present the basics of social defence and argue for a grassroots perspective, an offensive orientation and a revolutionary agenda. Chapter 2 gives a basic introduction to social defence; it may be skipped by those who are familiar with the ideas. Chapter 3 argues that it is futile to expect governments to implement social defence. Grassroots action towards social defence is required. In chapter 4, I review Steven Huxley's book on the Finnish constitutional insurgency in order to extract some insights for the development of social defence.

The military coups in Fiji are the focus of chapter 5. I describe the use of nonviolent action against the coups and argue that social defence should not be solely defensive. Nonviolent activists need to be willing to intervene against repression elsewhere. Chapter 7, on "revolutionary social defence," argues that the introduction of social defence may be a snowballing process analogous to the rise of the nation-state.

Chapters 8-14 are short discussions of links between social defence and different social structures or issues: patriarchy, the police, the environment, science policy, and political and economic systems. In each case, I spell out some of the radical implications of social defence for the organisation of society. Rather than being cautious, I've tried to see how far the argument can be taken. Therefore, I don't expect anyone to agree with all my conclusions, which are necessarily tentative. What I think is important is that these issues be discussed and, more importantly, brought into the planning of campaigns and initiatives. Undoubtedly, ideas about social defence will need to be revised in the light of practice.

There are quite a number of topics *not* addressed in this book which warrant treatment, such as industry, health, education, lesbian and gay rights, racism, immigration and nationalism. My intent is not to be comprehensive but to illustrate the far-reaching implications of social defence.

In chapters 8-14, I start with social defence and draw implications for all sorts of areas. Therefore it might seem that I'm putting social defence at the core of a radical programme. This is deceptive. Just the same sort of implications (or similar ones, anyway) could be drawn starting from one of the other areas—on one condition. The starting point must be people having the power to collectively shape their own lives. Social defence does this through organising communities to use nonviolent action against aggression and repression. Other starting points would do the same, such as feminism through empowering women or grassroots democracy through empowering communities. These chapters then are about drawing connections between a grassroots approach to social defence and grassroots approaches to other issues.

An assumption behind my analysis is that campaigns and strategies to introduce social defence should be linked to other campaigns and strategies towards a more egalitarian, participatory society. Social defence should be part of a *process* of social change.

2
Some basics

Defining social defence

Social defence is nonviolent community resistance to aggression as an alternative to military defence. It is based on widespread protest, persuasion, noncooperation and intervention in order to oppose military aggression or political repression. It uses methods such as boycotts, acts of disobedience, strikes, demonstrations and setting up alternative institutions.

Defining something is a political act, and so it is worthwhile looking at this definition of social defence as "nonviolent community resistance to aggression as an alternative to military defence." This definition says that the resistance is *community* resistance—not *national* resistance, which is the usual focus for military defence and for much thinking and writing about social defence. My view is that the focus should be on communities defending themselves and each other. Sometimes the communities will be nations, but often not.

Some activists prefer to define social defence as "nonviolent community resistance to aggression or oppression," thereby including defence against military aggression, defence against government oppression of local communities, and defence against male violence against women. Social defence, in this view, should be seen as nonviolent defence of the vital features of society—including human rights, local autonomy, and participation—against all oppressive forces.

I agree with the sentiments behind this broader orientation. But I think it is better to *define* social defence as an alternative to military defence and then to make links between this idea of social defence and other struggles against oppression. With the broader definition, social defence becomes almost the same as any community-based nonviolent action. This can lose the focus on the problems with military defence.

Of course, there is a very close connection between social defence and nonviolent action: social defence is based on the use of nonviolent action. Social defence means that the functions of the military are eliminated or replaced (or, at the very least, supplemented). There can be lots of nonviolent action in a community but, if the military is still present, there is the potential for waging war and carrying out repression.

Social defence is one of several different names that all mean about the same thing. The main ones are social defence, nonviolent defence, civilian-based defence and civilian defence. The different names do have different connotations. The expression "civilian-based defence" usually refers to nonviolent defence operating under direction of a government, whereas the expression "social defence" often refers to nonviolent defence based on grassroots initiatives.

Years ago, social defence was sometimes called "passive resistance." This gives the misleading impression that nonviolence is passive. The core of social defence is nonviolent *action*, and this includes strikes, fraternisation and setting up alternative institutions. There are also offensive measures to be taken, such as communications to undermine international and domestic support for the aggression. Social defence does *not* mean just sitting there and accepting whatever the aggressor inflicts.

"Social defence" and the main alternative terms include the word "defence." Ironically, this gives too narrow a view of what can be involved. The problem stems from the euphemism "military defence." Military forces are designed for war. Government departments of war changed their names to departments of defence in order to avoid the association with killing and destruction. "Defence" sounds much friendlier than war, the military or even "the army."

Nonviolence has the opposite problem: to many people it sounds weak. Social *defence* sounds purely defensive. That's why it's sometimes useful to talk of social *offence*.

Problems with military defence

War. Military forces can be used to attack as well as to defend. The weapons of modern war are designed for killing and injuring vast numbers of people, and also can devastate the environment. As long as armies and armaments are present, there is a possibility that they will be used. There are numerous wars occurring around the world today, causing enormous destruction and suffering. There is a continuing possibility of the extensive use of nuclear, chemical and biological weapons as well as increasingly deadly "conventional" weapons.

Since the development of planes and missiles, *everyone*—civilians as well as soldiers—is on the front line in a war. Social defence provides a way for *everyone* to take responsibility for defence, unlike military methods.

Arms races. Military methods often provoke others to use military methods, and they thus encourage the very threat they are intended to defend against. They create a climate of fear and also a belief that resolving conflict requires one side to dominate the other.

If a community relies on social defence and cannot launch a violent attack, then aggressors will find it harder to justify their reliance on violence. It is more difficult to convince soldiers of the justice of their government's war if they are attacking an unarmed opponent. Since social defence contains no military capability, nuclear attack and aerial bombardment become pointless and harder to justify.

Military repression. One of the greatest threats to freedom and democracy in many countries today is military forces. If military forces take over, who will stop them? Who guards the guardians?

With social defence, this problem does not arise, since social defence is based on popular participation and so removes the dependence on a professional defence force. The nonviolent methods used against a foreign aggressor can also be used against local military forces that try to take power.

Reduced democracy. Military forces are based on hierarchy and obedience. They train people to kill on command. This is contrary to the equality, questioning, mutual respect and dialogue that help promote a democratic society. The influence of military systems often inhibits or thwarts greater participation in the rest of society.

Social defence is much more compatible with a society based on equality and wide political participation.

Methods used in social defence

Gene Sharp, the leading researcher on nonviolent action, has identified 198 different *types* of nonviolent action and given examples of each one.[1] Sharp divides the methods of nonviolent action into three categories: symbolic actions, noncooperation, and intervention and alternative institutions.

Symbolic actions include:
formal statements (speeches, letters, petitions);
slogans, leaflets, banners;
rallies, protest marches, vigils, pickets;
wearing of symbols of opposition (such as the paper clips worn by Norwegian civilians during the Nazi occupation);
meetings, teach-ins.

Noncooperation includes:
social boycott, stay-at-home;
boycotts by consumers, workers, traders; embargoes;
strikes, bans, working-to-rule, reporting "sick";
refusal to pay tax or debts, withdrawal of bank deposits;
boycotts of government institutions;
disobedience, evasions and delays;
mock incapability ("misunderstandings," "mistakes").

Intervention and alternative institutions include:
fasts;
sit-ins, nonviolent obstruction and occupation;
destruction of information and records;
establishment of parallel institutions for government, media, transport, welfare, health and education.

---

1 Gene Sharp, *The Politics of Nonviolent Action* (Boston: Porter Sargent, 1973).

How does nonviolence work?

Social defence is based on the principle that no regime—whether a democracy or military dictatorship—can survive without the passive support or nonresistance of a large fraction of the population. In other words, all societies are built on consent, cooperation and obedience. Social defence is designed to systematically disrupt this consent, cooperation and obedience and replace it by noncooperation and disobedience.

If, in a business corporation or a government body, large numbers of the workers refuse to carry out instructions, set up their own communications systems and mobilise supporters from the outside, the top officials can do little about it.

This idea applies to military forces themselves. If only a few soldiers refuse orders, they can be arrested or shot: discipline can be maintained. But if large numbers refuse to cooperate, an army cannot function. This occurred during the Algerian Generals' Revolt (see below), in the collapse of the Russian army during World War I, during the Iranian Revolution (see below) and on many other occasions.

Actually, there are a lot of problems with the idea that regimes depend on consent that can be withdrawn. It doesn't take into account the complex ways in which power is exercised through social institutions such as bureaucracies, markets in goods and labour, patriarchy and the media. In most societies, it is no simple matter to "withdraw consent," because often there is no obvious "ruler" but rather a variety of complicated systems of social control. Nevertheless, although political theorists may turn up their noses at the consent theory of power, it is an excellent tool for community activists.[2]

How the idea of social defence developed

The idea of nonviolent resistance to aggression can be traced to a number of writers, including Henry David Thoreau, Leo Tolstoy, Elihu Burritt (a Christian pacifist), William James and Bertrand Russell. The campaigns led by Gandhi in South Africa and India

---

[2] Brian Martin, "Gene Sharp's theory of power," *Journal of Peace Research*, vol. 26, no. 2, 1989, pp. 213-222.

were important in developing the idea of a nonviolent alternative to war. Gandhi himself began advocating defence by nonviolent resistance in the 1930s. A number of writers were inspired by Gandhi and developed his ideas. In the 1930s, advocates of a nonviolent substitute for war included Richard Gregg, Bart de Ligt, Kenneth Boulding, Jessie Wallace Hughan and Krishnalal Shridharani.

Perhaps the first fully-fledged description of a national social defence system was that by Stephen King-Hall, a British writer and former naval officer, in his book *Defence in the Nuclear Age* published in 1958. King-Hall thought that British parliamentary democracy could be better defended from communism if the military were abolished and replaced by organised nonviolent resistance. King-Hall's treatment moved social defence onto the agenda as a pragmatic rather than just a moral alternative.

Shortly after this, the idea of social defence was developed by various researchers including Theodor Ebert in West Germany, Johan Galtung in Norway, Adam Roberts in Britain and Gene Sharp in the United States. These and other researchers have investigated past examples of nonviolent action, analysed the social conditions favourable for the implementation and success of social defence, and explored the possibilities for nonviolent action against invasions and coups.

Some members of peace groups, mainly in Europe, argued the case for social defence in the 1960s and 1970s. But in those decades social defence mostly remained at the level of argument: little or no practical action to mobilise communities for nonviolent resistance occurred. (One exception was the simulation on Grindstone Island in Canada in 1965, in which a group of Quakers role-played a military takeover and nonviolent resistance to it. The report on this exercise provides a number of valuable lessons.[3]) Also in the 1960s and 1970s, a few European governments evinced a limited interest in social defence by sponsoring studies.

In the 1980s there was increased interest in social defence. This was mainly due to the worldwide resurgence of the peace move-

---

3 Theodore Olson and Gordon Christiansen, *Thirty-one Hours: The Grindstone Experiment* (Toronto: Canadian Friends Service Committee, 1966).

ment and the consequent grappling by many people with the question, "If we disarm, how will we defend ourselves?" The prior studies and interest in social defence enabled it to be put on the list of "alternative defence policies."

A very important factor in the increased interest in social defence was the increasing numbers of people involved in nonviolent action. Nonviolent action has a long and inspiring history, but systematic preparation for this form of social action is relatively recent. It has been inspired especially by writings and sharing of skills from the Movement for a New Society in the United States and implemented in a major way in environmental campaigns in Europe, North America and Australia since the 1970s, especially against nuclear power.

Social defence is a well recognised option within peace movements in many countries, though there are major exceptions such as the United States. Many conscientious objectors have supported and spread the idea. There are some political parties in Europe, notably the German Greens, that have put social defence on their platforms. Nevertheless, social defence is still seen as an unorthodox and radical option even by many within the peace movement, and it is little known among the general public.

Historical examples

Illustrations from history can show how nonviolent action works and suggest the potential for social defence. Nevertheless, there are a number of reservations which are worth remembering.

Historical examples do not prove the case for social defence—or anything else. For every example of effective nonviolent action, another example could be provided of ineffective nonviolent action. Historical examples are like tools in a box. They can be useful for hammering points home, but if you try to build a grand edifice, someone else may be able to bring it tumbling down.

In many historical examples, nonviolent action was largely spontaneous. There was little preparation, no training and little planning. Therefore, these are not examples of an operational social defence system. They might be described as "spontaneous" or "ad hoc" social defence.

On the other hand, there is no need to be overly defensive about the examples. For every failure of nonviolent action, there is a failure of violent action (usually with far more horrendous consequences). It is useful to regularly make comparisons with historical examples of the use of violent action to put things in perspective.

The writing of history always involves interpretation and, therefore, value judgements. Some writers who favour the use of nonviolent action, such as Gene Sharp, present certain historical episodes in a different light than writers who assume that state power or class struggle or whatever is the crucial issue. This only serves to emphasise the point that historical examples are like tools in a box. Different people pick different tools and use them for different purposes, whether to show the potential power of nonviolence or the necessity of warfare.

Coups

Coups are often overlooked in the usual comparisons between having military forces and having none. Military regimes are, arguably, just as serious a problem as warfare itself. In such cases, militaries obviously are a cause rather than a solution to the problem.

Germany, 1920

On 13 March 1920 in Berlin, there was a putsch (military takeover) led by General von Lüttwitz. The extreme right-wing Dr Wolfgang Kapp became Chancellor. Commanders of the German army refused to support the elected government and took no action against the putsch. It was left to the people to take action.

Germany's Weimar republic had been set up after the country's defeat in World War I. The government in 1920 was led by President Friedrich Ebert. In the wake of the coup, the government fled from Berlin to Stuttgart, from which it encouraged resistance by noncooperation.

When the Kappists took over two pro-government newspapers, all Berlin printers went on strike. The Ebert government called for a general strike throughout Germany. Support for the strike was overwhelming, especially in Berlin, and included groups from most political and religious orientations.

Opposition by civil servants was also crucial in opposing the coup. Officials in government bureaucracies refused to head government departments under Kapp.

Noncooperation ran deep. Bank officials refused to honour cheques presented by Kappists unless they were signed by appropriate government officials. But not one such official would sign. Typists were not available to type proclamations for the Kappists.

Kapp foolishly alternated between making concessions and attempting crackdowns, neither of which produced support. As his weakness became more obvious, opposition increased. Some military units and the security police declared their support for the legal government. After only four days, Kapp resigned and fled. With the collapse of the putsch, the Ebert government could once again rely on the loyalty of the army.[4]

Comment

The Kapp putsch is an excellent example because of the many types of nonviolent action used. Especially important is the crucial role of legitimacy for any government. People usually think of a military regime as inevitably getting its way, but in practice it only does so when people routinely obey. Bank officials refusing to cash cheques is a wonderful example of the ordinary nature of much noncooperation.

The historical context is important in understanding the putsch. The Weimar republic was an attempt at setting up parliamentary democracy in the most difficult of situations. Not only was the economy in tatters, but there was serious opposition from both the right and left. There had nearly been a revolution in Germany in the aftermath of the war. The Ebert government could rely on the army, a bastion of conservatism, to oppose left-wing insurgency. On the other hand, the army generally did not oppose threats to the republic from the right, and most military leaders sat on the sidelines during the Kapp putsch. In the provinces, there was military action against the coup, but in Berlin popular action was necessary to defeat the putsch precisely because the army did nothing.

---

4 D. J. Goodspeed, *The Conspirators: A Study of the Coup d'État* (London: Macmillan, 1962).

Another element in the story of the putsch is the role of armed workers' groups in several parts of Germany. This left-wing armed struggle was an attempt at social revolution rather than just opposition to the coup. After the defeat of the putschists, the Ebert government used the army to smash the workers' opposition— including the general strike in Berlin, which was still continuing. General von Seeckt, who declined to oppose the coup, had no hesitation in using force against the workers.

It should also be remembered that the Weimar republic was followed by the Third Reich, in a transition that largely occurred through legal channels, including elections. The issue of the rise of the Nazis to power is a complex one. It is worth noting here that the Weimar republic regularly resorted to article 48 in its constitution, which essentially was a provision for martial law, in order to stop threats, especially from the left. This meant government repression of civil liberties, backed by the military. Clearly, there was no policy to develop the capacity of the population to use direct action to protect freedom and democracy (not to mention the overthrow of capitalism). The Kapp putsch triggered spontaneous mass nonviolent resistance, but this had no lasting consequences.

Algeria, 1961

Until 1962, Algeria was a colony of France. Beginning in 1954, an armed independence struggle was waged by Algerian nationalists against French settlers who were supported by French military forces. In April 1961, Charles de Gaulle, head of the French government, indicated that he was prepared to negotiate with the Algerian nationalists.

Leading sections of the French military in Algeria, who were strongly opposed to Algerian independence, staged a coup on 21-22 April 1961 in the city of Algiers. They were initially very successful, encountering little open resistance from loyal sections of the military. There was a possibility of a parallel putsch in France, or an invasion by French forces from Algeria.

Resistance to the coup developed rapidly. Trade unions and political parties called a one-hour general strike, and ten million workers joined. After some delay, de Gaulle, in a broadcast on 23 April, called for noncooperation with the coup by both civilians and troops. Although the rebel generals controlled the Algerian media, French broadcasts were picked up by many French soldiers in Algeria on their transistor radios.

In Algeria, many soldiers refused to cooperate with the coup. Many pilots flew their transport planes or fighters out of Algeria. Others faked mechanical problems. Many soldiers just stayed in their barracks. Others caused inefficiency in administration and communications.

After four days the coup disintegrated. Not a single shot had been fired at supporters of the coup.[5]

Comment

The special value of the example of the Algerian Generals' revolt is the many methods of noncooperation used by soldiers in Algeria. This is a good example to use when talking with military personnel! They, possibly more than anyone else, need to know of the power of noncooperation and of their responsibility to consider resisting rather than obeying orders.

It should be noted that the revolt and nonviolent resistance to it came towards the end of the long and bloody war for Algerian independence. The Algerian independence movement used ruthless methods, as did the French colonial army. As many as a million people were killed in the struggle. It might be asked whether a nonviolent liberation struggle could have achieved independence with less loss of life. One key point is that the French army could be relied upon to fight the Algerian nationalists—if they didn't, they would be killed. The limited loyalty of the French conscripts, and their low level of support for the war, was indicated by their noncooperation during the revolt. Arguably, the liberation struggle didn't make full use of potential dissent within the French army because of the polarising violence of the war.

Invasions

The usual justification for having military forces is to stop an invasion by another state's military forces. Therefore it is essential for advocates of social defence to give examples of what to do about invasions.

---

5 Adam Roberts, "Civil resistance to military coups," *Journal of Peace Research*, vol. 12, 1975, pp. 19-36.

The Ruhr, 1923

The Versailles treaty at the end of World War I required that Germany pay reparations to the victorious governments. Due to disastrous economic conditions, Germany defaulted on payments. In response, in January 1923 French and Belgian troops occupied the Ruhr, a region of Germany bordering France and Belgium. By this action, the French government also hoped to keep Germany weak economically and militarily.

Germany was unable to mount military resistance due to its small army and collapsing economy. The German government called instead for noncooperation. This struggle was called the *Ruhrkampf*.

There were many varieties of noncooperation carried out by employers, trade unionists, government workers and many others. There were rallies, strikes and boycotts. Railway workers refused to cooperate, and were dismissed. A French company was brought in to operate the railways, but the departing German workers sabotaged the equipment. The few trains that ran were boycotted. There was also resistance from civil servants, shopkeepers, trade unions and the press.

French authorities enacted severe penalties, with many fines, arrests, detentions, deportations, long prison sentences, confiscations, beatings, forced labour and shootings.

Some groups engaged in violent resistance, carrying out sabotage that led to deaths. This led to severe reprisals by the occupiers, undermined the unity of the resistance and weakened international support for it.

On 26 September 1923 the resistance was called off unconditionally by the German government. The German economy virtually collapsed in massive inflation partly caused by the printing of money to fund the resistance. But there were potent effects on the other side too. French public opinion was outraged by the brutality of the occupation, and this contributed to the fall of the French government in 1924.

Economically too, the occupation failed to achieve the extraction of resources for which it was originally designed. A revised schedule of reparations was arranged by an international commission. Occupation forces were withdrawn by June 1925.[6]

Comment

This is a good example to answer the question, "what if the enemy just occupied part of the country?" It is also a good illustration of how severe repression by an occupier can be counterproductive. Of course, France in 1923 was a "democratic" country, so that public opinion could exert considerable pressure. On the other hand, this was just five years after the 1914-1918 bloodletting of the western front, during which Germans were depicted in propaganda as cruel and inhuman huns. No doubt the nonviolence of the resistance contributed to the development of sympathy among the French public.

Czechoslovakia, 1968

In the 1960s, a number of reforms were made in Czechoslovakia which reduced the repressive aspects of communist rule. These moves—so-called "socialism with a human face"—were strongly supported by the Czechoslovak people, but bitterly opposed by the Soviet government.

On 20-21 August 1968, a military invasion of Czechoslovakia was launched by hundreds of thousands of troops from the Soviet Union and four other Warsaw Pact countries, with the expectation of installing a pro-Soviet government within a few days. Military resistance would have been bloody and futile, so the Czechoslovak government instructed the army not to resist the invasion.

The Czechoslovak people, from the political leadership to the workforce, united in spontaneous nonviolent resistance to the occupation. Noncooperation with the invaders was practised at all levels: by the president, by army officers, by shopkeepers, by farmers and even by secret police. People sat in front of tanks. Streets signs and house numbers were removed, and false information given out. People talked with the Soviet troops—who had been told they were invading to stop a capitalist takeover—and

---

6 Wolfgang Sternstein, "The Ruhrkampf of 1923: economic problems of civilian defence," in Adam Roberts (ed.), *The Strategy of Civilian Defence: Non-violent Resistance to Aggression* (London: Faber and Faber, 1967), pp. 106-135.

undermined their loyalty so rapidly that many had to be rotated out of the country within a matter of days.

Underground newspapers were published. Radio and television were broadcast (from changing locations), providing news and greatly helping the resistance. The announcers called strikes, gave tactical instruction on street confrontations, requested rail workers to slow the transport of Soviet equipment, cautioned against rumours and counselled nonviolence.

The nonviolent nature of the resistance undermined Soviet propaganda justifying the invasion. All acts of violence against the invaders received heavy Soviet media coverage. Indeed, some violent incidents apparently were staged by Soviet forces to discredit the resistance.

Due to the unified civilian resistance and to the demoralisation of Soviet troops, Soviet leaders offered reforms and other concessions. The Czechoslovak leaders, held in Moscow, were isolated from the resistance and were ignorant of the dynamics of nonviolent action. As a result, they did not really understand how effective the resistance was. Under extreme pressure, they made compromises. This demoralised the opposition. As the Czechoslovak position weakened, the Soviet forces consolidated the occupation, removing their "unnecessary" concessions.[7]

Comment

The Czechoslovak example is one of the best examples of nonviolent resistance to invasion because of the wide variety of effective methods used, especially fraternisation and the radio.

It is important to note that military resistance was not even tried. The Czechoslovak military sat on the sidelines, and Western forces likewise did nothing. Czechoslovak soldiers did provide some help to the resistance, for example in maintaining radio broadcasts.

The resistance can be judged a success or a failure depending on which comparison is made. The most active phase of resistance lasted only a week, but a puppet government was not installed until April 1969, eight months later. The resistance was important

---

7 Philip Windsor and Adam Roberts, *Czechoslovakia 1968: Reform, Repression and Resistance* (London: Chatto and Windus, 1969).

in causing a massive loss of Soviet credibility around the globe, especially in Western communist parties, at a minimal loss of life. Arguably, a violent resistance would not have been so successful in achieving this.

Toppling repressive governments

El Salvador, 1944

Maximiliano Hernández Martínez became the dictator of El Salvador in 1931. Although he introduced some valuable reforms, he ruthlessly crushed political opposition. In 1932, an armed uprising was brutally put down by the military, which executed many thousands of campesinos (small farmers) in reprisal.

Opposition developed in 1943, with leaflets and petitions. The government responded with increased censorship, arrests and other controls.

The opposition was stimulated by US government rhetoric of a fight for freedom and democracy against Nazism. Also important was outrage over constitutional changes allowing Martínez to serve a further six-year term as president.

On 2 April 1944, there was a military revolt, which was repressed harshly. This helped to trigger a nonviolent insurrection. University students took the lead and organised a student strike, which spread to high schools. Over a period of a few weeks, physicians and business people joined the strike, until virtually the entire country was at a standstill, including government offices, banks and railways. This was essentially a stay-at-home strike, which cut most services.

Police shot at some boys, killing one. As a result, large crowds surged onto the streets. On 8 May, Martínez agreed to resign, and he left the country three days later.

The military was not used against the insurrection. The unreliability of the soldiers had been shown by the 2 April revolt. The officer corps, which was loyal to Martínez, did not risk using the army against the population.

While the nonviolent action of the people was enough to bring down Martínez, it was not effective in ensuring a transition to a nonrepressive society. There was a military coup later in 1944. The years since have seen continued oppression of El Salvadoran people.[8]

Comment

This example is useful to counter the widespread perception that Latin American politics consists of right-wing military dictatorships, sometimes confronted by left-wing guerrillas. In Guatemala a few weeks later in 1944, stimulated by the example of El Salvador, the government was also toppled by nonviolent insurrection. In addition to these two cases, between 1931 and 1961 nine other Latin American presidents were ousted by nonviolent insurrection.

The case of El Salvador is also useful in illustrating that even in a police state there are opportunities for effective nonviolent resistance, although of course at a risk. A seemingly simple leaflet can be a very significant form of defiance. Wider noncooperation can be triggered by the process of open resistance, via strikes and further leaflets. If nothing is done by the government, others are emboldened to join in; repressive steps, on the other hand, can cause outrage and an expansion of resistance.

The limitation of the example is the poor outcome. There was no strategic plan behind the resistance: individuals and groups acted to bring down Martínez, but there was little thought about how to make the process lead to a stable and less repressive society.

This case illustrates the importance of making a link between nonviolent resistance to repression and a "positive programme" to create alternative institutions. Being *against* repression is not enough—action *for* a different system is also necessary.

Iran, 1978-1979

Iran under the Shah was an incredibly repressive state. The secret police were pervasive, and torture was used routinely to terrorise the population. Income from oil was used to finance a giant military machine. In addition, the Iranian government was actively supported by the United States government and was not opposed by the Soviet Union, Israel and most Arab states. Yet this

---

8 Patricia Parkman, *Nonviolent Insurrection in El Salvador: The Fall of Maximiliano Hernández Martínez* (Tucson: University of Arizona Press, 1988).

seemingly impregnable regime was overthrown without arms. There was horrific violence, almost all of it against unarmed opponents of the government.

The regime was riddled with corruption and out of touch with the needs of the people. Many groups opposed the Shah, from communists to Islamic fundamentalists.

Protest escalated in 1978. Troops opened fire on a crowd, killing several people. A mourning procession, held in Islamic tradition 40 days after the deaths, turned into a political protest, and troops were used again. Each time people were killed, this became a trigger for further protest 40 days later. Gradually more secular opponents joined the processions and religious demonstrations.

There were also massive strikes and go-slows in factories. Oil and power workers, crucial to the economy, were key participants. Eventually the economy ground to a halt, although food continued to be delivered.

The government was unable to stem the tide of opposition. The Shah vacillated between concessions that were unconvincing and repression that alienated more of the population. The Shah had created such a fawning entourage that he received no realistic advice. (Becoming a megalomaniac, out of touch with the people, is an occupational hazard for dictators.)

Martial law was declared in September 1978, but the cycle of demonstrations, killings of demonstrators and increased opposition continued. Strikes and closure of shops spread until the economy was in collapse.

The spiritual leader of the Islamic resistance, Ayatollah Khomeini, was in exile. Cassette tapes of Khomeini's speeches were smuggled into the country and distributed through the bazaars, which were key centres for opposition sentiment. Khomeini made calls for soldiers and police to desert.

Eventually the troops refused to obey and instead joined the revolution. The Shah fled the country and Khomeini became the new head of state.

Unfortunately, this revolution carried out without arms did not lead to a nonviolent society. The secular dictatorship of the Shah was replaced by a theocratic dictatorship which, after solidifying its power, was just as ruthless as its predecessor in stamping out dissent. Furthermore, the Islamic Republic waged a bloody war with Iraq for most of a decade, leading to many more deaths than those that occurred under the Shah.[9]

Comment

The Iranian example is an outstanding one for showing that unarmed resistance can work against the most repressive regime. It is a risky example because of the widespread loathing of the Islamic Republic in the West. (This loathing may be well deserved, but it is partly due to a systematic campaign of vilification by Western governments, supported by news media. The repressive regime of the Shah was a key element in Western military planning, so its abuses of human rights were largely ignored.)

If you are able to make the distinction between the nonviolent methods used in the revolution and the repressive regime that came to power after the revolution, then this is a useful example. After all, military forces were not used to undermine the Shah: they were supporting his rule. There were some left-wing guerrilla opponents of the Shah, but they were small in number, infiltrated by state agents, and served to justify government repression. It was the power of the people that won the day.

The opposition was not entirely nonviolent. As well as demonstrations, strikes, go-slows and closure of businesses, there were many riots, often triggered by shootings by soldiers. The key point is that armed struggle against the Shah played almost no role.

It is worth noting that the loyalty of the regime's troops is a key to revolution, whether violent or nonviolent. The nonviolence of the opposition helped undermine the loyalty of the troops.

Some might argue that tens of thousands of people killed is a high price to pay. But this is a relatively small figure compared to many revolutions won by guerrilla struggle.

The Iranian Revolution can also be used to make the point that nonviolent action, as a tool, does not guarantee creation of a nonviolent society. As in the case of El Salvador, it is crucial that non-

---

9 David H. Albert (ed.), *Tell the American People: Perspectives on the Iranian Revolution* (Philadelphia: Movement for a New Society, 1980); Fereydoun Hoveyda, *The Fall of the Shah* (London: Weidenfeld and Nicolson, 1980).

violent action against repression be linked with action to create nonviolent social institutions.

Severe repression

What about ruthless invaders who just keep killing people at the least hint of resistance? What can be done to stop a programme of total extermination? How can social defence possibly work against repressive regimes?

Real-life dictatorships are not as all-powerful as might be imagined. Under the brutal military regimes in Argentina and Chile, many individuals continued to openly express opposition in the workplace, in public protests and in the media. Protests have shaken the harsh regimes in South Korea and Burma. If nonviolent resistance could be prepared for and expanded, then dictatorships would be difficult to sustain.

For example, consider the courageous stand of publisher Jacobo Timerman in Argentina, who maintained his newspaper's open resistance until he was arrested and tortured. An international campaign led to his release and he wrote about his experiences in a powerful book. His efforts were among those that contributed to the collapse of the generals' regime in the country.[10] Such examples show how the withdrawal of consent can undermine even a ruthless dictatorship.

My friend Ralph Summy argues that the question "What about severe repression?" is the wrong one. Ruthlessness—namely, the psychology of the ruler—is not the key factor.

The real question is how to make sure that the ruler is dependent in some way on the nonviolent resisters. This might be economic dependence; it could be the influence of family members who know people in the resistance; or it could be a sense of ethnic or cultural identity. If there is a dependency relationship, then the ruler will encounter great obstacles if severe repression is used. But if there isn't some direct or indirect connection between the two sides, then

---

10 Jacobo Timerman, *Prisoner Without a Name, Cell Without a Number*, translated from the Spanish by Toby Talbot (New York: Vintage, 1982).

even a fairly benevolent ruler may do really nasty things. Dependency, not attitude, is the key.[11]

International support is important too, since there are many opportunities for nonviolent resistance to repressive regimes from people on the outside. Later chapters argue the importance of social *offence*.

The methods and tactics used in social defence need to be specially chosen if repression is harsh. More use can be made of quiet "mistakes" in carrying out tasks and "misunderstandings" of orders. Preparation in advance is crucial for things such as shutting down factories, protecting dissidents, providing food and shelter for survival, maintaining communications and exposing repression to the world. When support for the resistance becomes widespread, open defiance becomes possible.

Gene Keyes, a social defence researcher, provides a more uncomfortable response to the question about severe repression. He notes that it is seldom easy to stop a ruthless invader or ruler, whether using violence or not. Military planners routinely anticipate thousands or millions of casualties in opposing the enemy, most obviously in the case of waging a nuclear war. Social defence planning, says Keyes, therefore must also prepare for heavy casualties. If people are not willing to make the sacrifice, then perhaps they should think again about whether resistance is worth the cost.[12]

The question of whether a social defence should be prepared to "accept" heavy casualties is a fundamental challenge, and has hardly been discussed. Of course, advocates of military methods seldom discuss this either—Herman Kahn did so in his book *On Thermonuclear War* and caused an uproar—but have implicitly "agreed" to "accept" heavy casualties. The issue of heavy casualties *seems* more acute for social defence than military defence. One reason is that people misunderstand nonviolence to mean no violence at all.

---

11 Johan Galtung, *Nonviolence and Israel/Palestine* (Honolulu: University of Hawaii Institute for Peace, 1989).
12 Gene Keyes, "Heavy casualties and nonviolent defense," *Philosophy and Social Action*, vol. 17, nos. 3-4, July-December 1991, pp. 75-88.

Nonviolence against the Nazis?

Supporters of nonviolence frequently are asked, "What about the Nazis?" This question assumes that the experience of Nazi Germany is a refutation of nonviolence. Well, what about them?

To begin, it is important to realise that throughout most of the Third Reich the Nazi regime relied on support, in many cases ardent support, from a significant fraction of the German people. Many people in other countries were admirers of the Nazis as well. Supporters of military methods tended to be especially favourable to them.

Nevertheless, throughout the rule of the Nazis, there *was* a German opposition to Hitler. This internal opposition was not fostered by the Allies, nor has it been given sufficient credit by postwar writers.[13]

Nonviolence against the Nazis was only tried occasionally and unsystematically. There was effective nonviolent resistance in several countries, including Norway, Denmark and the Netherlands. In Germany itself, on several occasions public protest led to changes in policies, as when in 1941 church leaders publicly condemned Hitler's programme of "mercy killing" of institutionalised people with disabilities and when in 1943 protests by non-Jewish wives of arrested Jewish men led to their release. When there was active resistance to Nazi genocides, especially by political and church leaders in occupied countries, many fewer people were killed. According to Helen Fein, a leading scholar on genocide, "German instigation and organization of extermination usually succeeded because of the lack of counterauthorities resisting their plans, not because of their repression of such resistance."[14]

There was no concerted attempt from *outside* Germany to undermine the Nazis using nonviolent methods. Stephen King-Hall gives a telling account of how he tried futilely as late as 1939 to drum up British government support for a campaign to undermine

---

13   Hans Rothfels, *The German Opposition to Hitler* (London: Oswald Wolff, 1961).
14   Helen Fein, *Accounting for Genocide: National Responses and Jewish Victimization during the Holocaust* (New York: Free Press, 1979), p. 90.

the German people's support for Hitler.[15] There has been no further study on this issue, so it remains a possibility that concerted nonviolent attack from around the world could have undermined or restrained the Nazi regime.

The case of the Nazis should not be removed from its historical context. It is unfair to set up a worst case—the rise of a ruthless regime and its solidification of power—and *then* expect nonviolence to be a solution. Social defence, before it can be fairly assessed, needs its own process of development and solidification. Nevertheless, if advocates of social defence use historical examples that they choose, they need to be able to respond to examples chosen by others.

If nonviolence didn't succeed against the Nazis, neither did violence. The normal assumption underlying the Nazi example is that only violence—namely the Allied war effort—would have worked against the Nazis in a period less than decades.

The war by Western governments was against German military and political expansion, not against the ruthless system of fascism alone. The Allies in World War II did not attempt to topple the fascist regimes in Spain and Portugal. After the war, the Allies allowed or encouraged many fascists to obtain positions of power.[16] Numerous Nazi war criminals were employed by US spy agencies.[17] Essentially, the war was about power politics, not justice and freedom. Western military strength has not been used against numerous dictatorial regimes around the world, but instead has frequently been used to prop them up.[18]

Nazi genocidal politics were *not* the reason why Western governments waged war against Nazi Germany. There is ample historical evidence that easy opportunities to disrupt death camp

---

15 Stephen King-Hall, *Total Victory* (London: Faber and Faber, 1941), appendix 3.
16 Tom Bower, *Blind Eye to Murder: Britain, America and the Purging of Nazi Germany—A Pledge Betrayed* (London: Andre Deutsch, 1981).
17 Christopher Simpson, *Blowback: America's Recruitment of Nazis and its Effects on the Cold War* (New York: Weidenfeld and Nicolson, 1988).
18 Noam Chomsky and Edward S. Herman, *The Political Economy of Human Rights* (Boston: South End Press, 1979).

operations were passed over by the Allied governments. The policy was explicitly to win the war first and stop genocidal killing afterwards. The Allies minimised any association of their cause with that of the Jews.[19]

Indeed, genocide has often been permitted to proceed with no military intervention by "non-ruthless" governments. The Turkish government's extermination of the Armenians in 1915, Stalin's purges in the 1930s and the Cambodian exterminations from 1975 to 1979 are major examples where military forces in other countries stood by and did nothing. Of course, the killings were carried out by, or with the support of, the militaries in the countries where they occurred.[20]

Finally, several commentators have pointed out that the Nazi extermination of the Jews and other stigmatised groups did not begin until after the war began. In effect, the war provided a brutalising environment conducive to the killings as well as a cover for them. Much of the blame for Nazi genocide can be attributed to the war itself.

Conclusion

In this chapter I've raised some of the basic issues about social defence, partly through recounting and commenting on historical examples. There are, of course, many other questions that people raise about social defence. It is not my aim here to make a comprehensive case for social defence. Besides, for most people, arguments alone are insufficient. Personal experiences are a necessary part of understanding how it might work.

Instead, I assume that social defence is worth investigating and developing further, in a variety of ways and in a number of different directions. As part of this process, in the following chapters I outline a radical agenda for social defence.

---

19   Martin Gilbert, *Auschwitz and the Allies* (London: Michael Joseph, 1981).
20   Leo Kuper, *Genocide* (Harmondsworth: Penguin, 1981).

3
Elite reform or grassroots initiative?

If social defence is to be introduced on a large scale, how will it come about? Will it be introduced by government and military elites who have become convinced that it is a better method of defence? Or will it be introduced by the initiatives of many individuals and local groups, often in the face of elite resistance?

These questions cannot be answered simply by referring to past history. There is yet no substantive example of a community which has systematically organised its members and its political, economic and technological systems to operate social defence. True, there are a number of suggestive historical examples such as the Kapp Putsch and Czechoslovakia 1968. But all such efforts have been organised spontaneously. Planned social defence has yet to be organised on a major scale.

For those who would like to see social defence researched, developed and implemented, the question is, what is the best way to help this come about? Here I describe two general approaches for introducing social defence: elite reform and grassroots initiative. I argue that relying on elites to introduce social defence is unreliable and also undercuts its potential to challenge the roots of war. By contrast, promoting social defence at the grassroots provides a much sounder basis for long-term success, and also provides valuable connections with other social struggles which contribute to overturning the war system and related systems of power and exploitation.

28   Elite reform or grassroots initiative?

Elite reform

Some prominent proponents of social defence have pitched their arguments towards elites, especially state bureaucrats. Their aim has been to win over influential leaders by showing that social defence is more effective than military defence in attaining at least some of the explicit goals of governments and military establishments.

The arguments for social defence are good ones. For example, races to develop ever more devastating weapons for "defence" decrease rather than increase people's security, whereas social defence, which cannot be used to launch deadly attacks, avoids this paradox. Military defence provides the basis for military coups and military dictatorships which repress the very people who are supposed to be defended; social defence avoids the dilemma of "who guards the guardians?" by turning the people into their own nonviolent guardians against both external and internal threats.

Gene Sharp is the best example of an advocate of social defence who aims his arguments at governmental and military elites. His books *Making Europe Unconquerable* and *Civilian-Based Defense*,[1] which are effective and valuable arguments for social defence, seem to be aimed mainly at policy makers in government and the military.

Let me make it clear that I think that Gene Sharp's scholarship and writing is extremely valuable. I routinely recommend it to many people. But that does not provide any reason to refrain from "friendly criticism" of some of his underlying assumptions.

Sharp assumes that the reason for present military policies is that people, both policy makers and the general population, are not aware that there is a viable alternative defence policy without the extreme dangers of mass warfare. Sharp gives hardly a hint that there might be other reasons for the reliance on

---

1 Gene Sharp, *Making Europe Unconquerable: The Potential of Civilian-based Deterrence and Defense* (Cambridge, MA: Ballinger, 1985); Gene Sharp with the assistance of Bruce Jenkins, *Civilian-Based Defense: A Post-Military Weapons System* (Princeton: Princeton University Press, 1990).

military means than the perceived need to defend against the "enemy."

In my view,[2] military establishments are created and sustained for purposes other than just defence and security. Military establishments and associated industry and government bureaucracies have strong organisational and economic interests in their continued existence even in the absence of external threats or the presence of "superior" defence alternatives. More fundamentally, the state is premised on the monopoly over what is claimed to be legitimate violence within a territory, within a system of competing states. It is not feasible to dismantle the military system of organised potential for violence without also undermining the dominant power structures within states, including the power of capitalist and bureaucratic elites.

So it is really out of the question to expect state elites to introduce social defence simply by convincing them that it is logically a better system for the interests of the people. In most cases, the beliefs of state elites reflect the power structures in which they operate. Knowledge and logic alone can do little to undermine these structures.

If military defence were really there to defend against "the enemy," the US and other Western governments would be *massively* reducing their arsenals and expenditures in the wake of the collapse of state socialism in the Soviet Union and Eastern Europe. It is safe to predict that this will not occur. New excuses for maintaining military strength will be conjured up, such as "instability" due to resurgent nationalism, newly demonised dictators such as Saddam Hussein of Iraq, the drug trade, or internal unrest and subversion.

Elites might well give more consideration to social defence if popular pressure became greater. Some advocates of social defence indeed favour development of popular support for social defence as a way to influence elite decision-makers to take it more seriously. From the point of view of elites, popular pressure might make social defence more attractive as an elite reform. Sharp recognises this when he suggests that governments might adopt social defence measures to "mollify" a strong peace movement.

---

2 Brian Martin, *Uprooting War* (London: Freedom Press, 1984).

If governments brought in social defence as a reform, it would almost certainly be done in those ways most compatible with existing institutions. What would this mean for social defence?

First, social defence would be seen as a contribution to *national* defence, supporting the interest of a particular state within the existing framework of competing states. Sharp does not deal with social defence except as national defence.

Second, social defence would be administered from the top. Although popular participation is intrinsic to the operation of social defence, participation can be either organised and designed by those participating in it or manipulated and controlled from above. Elite-sponsored social defence could well be organised and run by a professional corps of experts and leaders, with the populace participating in accordance with the plans and directions of the professionals. This sort of social defence would be relatively undemocratic. It is even possible to imagine conscription for social defence service, which would be a travesty of nonviolent action.

Third, elite-sponsored social defence would be integrated with other methods of defence, including continuation of military defence. Instead of becoming a replacement for military defence, social defence would become a supplement. Sharp sees this as the most likely path for introduction of social defence (although he gives many examples of the dangers of mixing violent and nonviolent resistance). This would pre-empt more radical initiatives for popularly organised social defence. In terms of infrastructure—communications, transport, factory production—social defence would depend on the existing facilities which are geared to control by elites.

Social defence which is organised by professionals for national defence as a supplement to military defence could actually serve to contain popular action for social change. The military establishment, through its influence over social defence plans and knowledge of avenues for popular action, might find itself more able to control the populace. Since the elite-sponsored social defence would be oriented towards external enemies, it would be harder to use against domestic repression. Because of the top-down control, it would be relatively easy for elites to reduce overall commitment to social defence. Finally, elite sponsorship, by giving the *appearance* that social defence is being officially promoted, would reduce initiative from below. In essence, power over the development of social defence would have been put in the hands of those most likely to oppose its radical potential.

In summary, elite-sponsored social defence would have a minimal impact on dominant institutions. The state system and the necessity for its defence would remain a central premise. Popular participation would be under the control of elites and professionals, and the military system would not be challenged in any fundamental way. This sort of elite reform could coopt social defence in the same way that demands for workers' control have been partially coopted by limited forms of worker participation and demands for women's liberation have been partially coopted by promoting some women into high positions within otherwise unchanged institutions.

It should be clear that I don't see attempts to convince or apply pressure to elites as the best way to promote social defence. If any headway in this direction is made at all, it is likely to be to achieve a form of social defence lacking its most important democratic features and providing no real threat to established institutions which underlie the war system.

Grassroots initiative

Another way to promote social defence is through grassroots initiatives. This means that groups of people in suburbs, factories, offices, schools, churches, farming communities and military forces would take the initiative to prepare for and implement social defence.

Small steps in this direction began in the 1980s. There are groups and individuals active in various parts of the world, such as Australia, Austria, Italy and the Netherlands.

There are many possible things to do. In factories, for example, workers might teach each other how to use equipment and also how to disable it so far as outsiders were concerned. They could plan decision-making procedures for crisis situations and organise communications networks for coordinating their own efforts with other community groups.

For workers to make these preparations would require considerable self-education about social defence. The process of developing a social defence system would itself be an important component of the education process. Once preparations were under way, they could be tried out in role-playing exercises and, eventually, with large-scale simulations in which the factories were shut down to prevent aggressors using them or, instead, used to produce products useful to the nonviolent resistance.

In the longer term, factory workers could begin pushing for changes in the social and technological systems. Greater use of job rotation and shop-floor decision-making would develop the skills of the workers and make them more effective in resisting aggression. Flattening wage differentials and reducing management prerogatives would help reduce inequalities and antagonisms between sections of the workforce which might be used by aggressors to undermine worker solidarity. Decentralising production and converting wasteful or harmful production to production for human needs would increase the value of the workers' labour for community needs, and in many cases reduce its value to aggressors, as in the case of converting military-related production. Developing wider communication and decision-making forms, such as workers' councils, would provide a solid organisational basis for social defence.

This example of a grassroots initiative for social defence illustrates several features different from the likely direction of elite-sponsored social defence. First, the orientation would be much more to defence at the community level rather than only at the national level. Since the state is a key feature of the war system, this community focus is much more suitable for putting social defence into a wider antiwar strategy.

Second, a grassroots approach would lead to a much more democratic and self-reliant social defence system. Because people would be involved themselves in developing social defence, they would be much more committed to it. The defence would be stronger because it would be less reliant on professionals and official leaders. Also, to the extent that reorganisation of social and technological systems occurred, the basis for war-making by political and economic elites would be undercut.

Third, social defence developed through grassroots initiatives would be much more potent against attacks by state elites. Self-reliance developed at the grassroots could be better mobilised

Elite reform or grassroots initiative? 33

against a repressive government or against a coup supported by government leaders—a situation only poorly addressed by Sharp.

Finally, and most importantly, many more links would be made with other social movements. For example, the methods of nonviolent resistance developed by workers to oppose outside aggressors could be used against oppressive employers. Indeed, nonviolent action is regularly used against employers, and this provides the best motivation for developing workers' skills and experience in nonviolent struggle. Other links are treated in chapters 8-14.

A grassroots approach to social defence implies that social defence is not just a desirable goal, to be implemented in whatever way possible. Rather, social defence would become an organising tool. Organising of communities could be based around the development of social defence skills and preparations, since this would require promotion of increased local democracy, self-reliance and participation.

There are many obstacles to social defence organised from the grassroots. Factory workers promoting greater shop-floor decision-making power will be strongly opposed by employers, by allied state bureaucracies, and also by many trade union elites. Historically, elite opposition to strong workers' movements has relied ultimately on military force. Specifying this array of forces highlights the close connections between the war system and other systems of political and economic exploitation. A grassroots approach to social defence can only succeed if it is part of a wider challenge to oppressive institutions such as patriarchy, capitalism and the state.

There is a long way to go before social defence becomes adopted as an organising tool in very many places. But once teething problems are sorted out—and this will take many years, if not decades—there is no reason why rapid expansion in the use of social defence could not occur. Certainly this is what has happened in other social movements in their use of nonviolent methods. One hopeful sign is the dramatic use in recent years of nonviolence against repressive regimes in the Philippines, Palestine, Eastern Europe and elsewhere. As more grassroots initiatives get going, they will be much harder to stop than any elite-sponsored systems.

Two approaches to the promotion of social defence

	Elite reform	Grassroots action
Implementation	Governments	Mass action
Key target audience	Governments and military officials	Social movements
Domain of defence	National	Local, national, transnational
Social context	Social defence as a functional alternative	Social defence as part of wider social change
Key promoters	Academic researchers	Community activists
Argument, justification	Rational superiority of social defence to military defence	Commitment to non-violence, participation, social justice

Reservations about research

Gene Sharp says that serious consideration of social defence "is more likely to be advanced by research, policy studies, and strategic analyses of its potential than by a 'campaign' being launched advocating its immediate adoption."[3] Sharp's view is flawed on two counts. First, activists who campaign for social defence do not demand its "immediate adoption," but rather foresee a gradual but punctuated process, just as Sharp does. Second, and more serious in its implications, is Sharp's view that research is more useful than "campaigns." Sharp clearly wants to distance himself from the peace movement, and indeed he hardly mentions it in his books. His concern is with so-called policy studies and policy-makers, the word "policy" here referring only to government-level activity.

The history of social movements shows that popular action is the key to social change, not the logical arguments of experts with the ear of elites. The anti-slavery movement would never have made much progress simply by trying to convince slave-owners that it was more economically efficient to have a free labour force. Nor

---

3 Sharp, 1985, p. ix. See also p. 64.

would the women's movement have made much progress simply by trying to convince individual men that sexual equality was more in keeping with the highest precepts of human civilisation. Similarly, all the available evidence shows the futility of relying on governments to abolish the war system.

Undoubtedly, it is important to popular movements for there to be intellectuals who argue their case, and often these intellectuals prefer to set themselves apart from the movements which use their material. Sharp's writings are immensely valuable to social activists, who will continue to read and refer to his work even if he does not consider their activities worthy of mention. That's all a part of the typical dynamic of social movements and intellectuals.

It is understandable that Sharp, a researcher, should advocate more research. But there is not really such a great disjunction between research and action as implied by Sharp. Sharp's writings are actually effective tools in nonviolent struggles against oppression and war. Conversely, many campaigns are very effective research tools. Usually the best way to obtain knowledge is to become involved in social action rather than waiting on the sidelines for it to occur.

Reservations about voting

In Switzerland in 1989, a citizens' initiative to abolish the army obtained more than one third of the vote. This was an astounding performance considering the limited resources of the group Switzerland Without an Army and the active opposition of the government. The proponents of the initiative hope that eventually armies may be abolished by popular mandate.

This approach is based on persuading people that armies are counterproductive and unnecessary, and using the mechanism of the citizens' initiative to bring about institutional change. The advantage of this approach is that it brings the issues to the general population and puts decision-making power in their hands. But it has several disadvantages.

First, only some countries make provision for citizens' initiatives. Second, a campaign to get people to vote a certain way does not give them skills or experience for undertaking direct action. Third, and most importantly, there is no guarantee that even a majority vote will lead to actual abolition of the army, since there is no force, aside from the law, to make the government obey the vote. Popular direct action would be needed to implement a vote to abolish the army. How better to promote the capacity and preparedness for such action than through preparation for social defence?

One of the difficulties with promoting many of the "alternative defence" options, such as "defensive military defence" and armed neutrality as well as citizens' initiatives to abolish the army, is that they depend on politicians and state bureaucrats for implementation. Social activists are ultimately reduced to applying pressure on elites.

Combining methods

In practice, opponents of war use a variety of methods: community organising, lobbying elites, working through political parties, total resistance to military service, peace education, research, mediation, conflict resolution, voting, direct action and many others. Complete reliance on any single method is a mistake.

If *everyone* focussed on the grassroots, then a bit of lobbying of lonely elites would be called for. But this is pretty unlikely! In my view, the main priority should be grassroots initiatives. Relying on elites is easy, familiar and filled with traps. Grassroots methods need more development. Who will take the initiative? Can grassroots activity be organised on a regular and sound basis without being captured by new elites? What is the motivation for initiatives: enemy threats or local problems? These are difficult questions. The answers can only come through experience with grassroots initiatives.

Concluding comment

Sharp says that social defence should be "transpartisan": "no peace or pacifist group or radical political organization should identify itself as the prime advocate of civilian-based defense."[4] I agree that social defence should be developed by a range of organisations and not tied to one tendency. But neither is it likely, à la

---

4 Sharp, 1990, p. 124.

Sharp, to be a neutral technique that can be taken up by just anybody with equal ease and value. Popular nonviolent action has much more in common with grassroots democracy than with government and military hierarchy.

Sharp says that social defence should be "presented on the basis of its potential utility—without ideological baggage." Sorry, Gene. Your approach is ideological too.

Social movements have often come to grief when reliance has been put on elites to implement policy. Activists cannot afford to wait for research and action from the top. It would be especially ironic if social defence, which by its nature is ideally suited for grassroots initiatives, were to become another captive and casualty of elite policy-making.

4
Steven Huxley and "nonviolent" struggle

The struggle by the Finnish people against imposition of controls by the Russian Empire from 1899 to 1905 is commonly cited as an excellent example of nonviolent struggle. But is it really that straightforward? Not according to Steven Huxley in his book *Constitutionalist Insurgency in Finland*.[1]

The Finnish story seems straightforward. In 1899 the Tsar issued a manifesto claiming the right to enact laws, on issues affecting Russian interests, without the consent of the Finnish Diet. (In 1809 Finland, previously a dependency of Sweden, became a Grand Duchy in the Russian Empire, with a considerable degree of autonomy.) A programme of Russification was initiated. In 1900, Russian was designated the official language. In 1901, a decree disbanded the Finnish army and demanded conscription of Finns into the Russian army.

The response was a mobilisation of resistance in Finland, with meetings, journals, petitions and noncooperation. The attempt to conscript Finns failed due to a boycott. Thus nonviolence proved effective against Russian oppression. This, at least, is the usual story. Huxley's book shows that the full picture is much more complex.

---

1 Steven Duncan Huxley, *Constitutionalist Insurgency in Finland: Finnish "Passive Resistance" against Russification as a Case of Nonmilitary Struggle in the European Resistance Tradition* (Helsinki: Finnish Historical Society, 1990).

Constitutionalist Insurgency in Finland is filled with provocative insights for both supporters and critics of nonviolent action. My aim here is to draw on a few of Huxley's points to raise issues for today's nonviolent activists.

The book has several levels. The most obvious pertains to the historical events of the Finnish Constitutionalist insurgency. Huxley analyses the views of leading thinkers, the arguments presented at the time for and against the insurgency, and the nature of Finnish society.[2]

A second level or dimension to the book is Huxley's argument about the Finnish struggle: "Around the turn of the twentieth century, the Finnish Constitutionalists developed one of the most ideologically and technically sophisticated and successful versions of European passive resistance and nonmilitary struggle" (p. 253). The dynamics of the struggle are elucidated in some detail.

Yet, doesn't this sound just like what we are used to calling nonviolent action? Indeed. But Huxley aims to show that calling the Finnish resistance a case study of "nonviolent action" is potentially misleading. As a long prelude to the Finnish case study, he analyses ideas about nonviolence and passive resistance. As Huxley discusses the Finnish case, he adds many arguments about modern nonviolence theory.

A final level to the book is a continual critique of historical interpretations. The Finnish case, like many other accounts of nonviolent action, has been turned into a myth, both by those participating in the Finnish struggle and by today's writers. Whenever Huxley recounts the views of some participant or historian, he invariably accompanies this with a critical assessment of biases, social interests and contrary interpretations. Rather than presenting a history, he is presenting a sophisticated argument within a particular historical context.

All of this results in a considerable conceptual complexity to the book. It contrasts greatly with the more familiar accounts of

---

2 If you are looking for a convenient account of the struggle, you would be better advised to consult an encyclopaedia, such as the *Encyclopaedia Britannica*. Much more detail is provided by the *Great Soviet Encyclopedia*, with its own set of biases. Huxley assumes a familiarity with the basic events of Finnish history.

nonviolent struggles which are stories with inspiring messages and, frequently, happy endings.[3] Huxley has a much more complex and challenging message and he forces the reader to work much harder to decipher it.

Let me now turn to some lessons that can be drawn from *Constitutionalist Insurgency in Finland*.

Be wary of historical examples

Huxley's analysis of the Finnish resistance clearly shows that the struggle was much more complex than the usual idea of valiant defenders of freedom opposing a ruthless oppressor.

Finland had long had a dependent relation to the Russian Empire (and also to Sweden). What happened beginning in 1899 was an increased pressure to integrate the society into the Empire. This was not military invasion or ruthless oppression. The means used by the Tsar included edicts and granting more power to the governor general of Finland. The struggle was social and political, not military.

Yet the Finnish case is commonly cited by proponents of nonviolent struggle. Huxley thinks that it is illegitimate to use the Finnish struggle in order to conclude that nonviolent methods could be used to totally replace military defence (though he thinks they might in certain circumstances).

Let it be clear: Huxley does not reject social defence outright. He merely says the Finnish struggle does not provide a good precedent for it. In his words, "Apparently it is an entirely vain endeavour to try to extrapolate from historical cases or derive from theoretical construction a form of defensive power politics which if adopted by a community which has renounced the use of organized violence would render it inviolable or even less violable than military defense" (p. 265). Huxley believes that social defence cannot be proved to be a "functional equivalent" to military defence, since its functions do not entirely overlap with those of military defence.

---

3 See for example Robert Cooney and Helen Michalowski (eds.), *The Power of the People: Active Nonviolence in the United States* (Culver City, CA: The Power of the People Publishing Project, 1977); Dick Scott, *Ask that Mountain: The Story of Parihaka* (Auckland: Heinemann/Southern Cross, 1975).

Huxley also discusses, briefly, the American struggle for independence, and reaches the same conclusion. Some scholars have argued that the struggles from 1765-1775 operated as a nonviolent defence system.[4] Huxley accepts that the American colonists mobilised socially, politically and economically against social, political and economic oppression, but says that this should not be seen as a substitute for war. Certainly the colonists did not conceive of their methods as a replacement for military struggle.

For me, the important point is that drawing lessons from historical examples is likely to be contentious at best and more often plain misleading. In giving talks about social defence, I commonly use examples such as the 1920 Kapp Putsch, the Ruhrkampf of 1923, the 1961 Algerian Generals' Revolt and the 1968 Czechoslovak resistance to the Soviet invasion. Yet, I now ask myself, how often do I "forget" to mention the important qualification that such examples do not show the viability of social defence as a complete "functional equivalent" for armed struggle, but only that nonviolent methods have been taken up, with more or less success, in specified historical circumstances?

Of course, misuse of history is commonplace. How often do we hear that World War II shows that violence was necessary to stop Hitler or that the absence of nuclear war since 1945 shows the success of nuclear deterrence? But just because supporters of military methods routinely use mythical history as propaganda is no excuse for critics to do the same. It hardly makes sense to try to create a more nonviolent society on the basis of misleading ideas about past struggles.

What is Huxley's alternative? Does he think that military defence is essential, or only that one should not draw unjustified arguments from history? This is not clear from his book. Some might dismiss his criticisms as being purely negative. In my view, this would be unwise.

Another way forward is to note that Huxley's critique applies only to the idea that social defence provides a functional alternative to military defence, namely the "elite reform" perspective

---

4 Walter H. Conser, Jr., Ronald M. McCarthy, David J. Toscano and Gene Sharp (eds.), *Resistance, Politics, and the American Struggle for Independence, 1765-1775* (Boulder: Lynne Rienner, 1986).

discussed in the previous chapter. He believes that eliminating organised violence, if it is possible, will require major changes in society, a view quite compatible with social defence as a grassroots initiative.[5]

Not all nonviolent action supports a just cause

The struggle between Russia and Finland involved no physical violence on either side. Of course, the overwhelming military power lay with Russia. But Finland was not high among the concerns of the Empire, which was confronted with a variety of challenges. The Constitutionalist insurgency that Huxley analyses was concerned with questions of formal status. The Russian ruler tried to impose controls on Finland that, in some interpretations, had legal sanction; Finnish resisters tried to maintain the de facto independence of Finland, justifying it with their own interpretation of constitutional matters. The conflict, then, could be called a nonviolent struggle between a regime and part of its empire.

Supporters of nonviolent action commonly refer to the Finnish resistance as nonviolent. But they do not refer to the Russian government's actions as nonviolent. Why not? Because, from today's vantage point, it is common to identify Russia as an oppressive imperialist power and Finland as a valiant nation seeking independence. There is an unstated assumption that nonviolent action always supports a just cause. Huxley makes this point well:

> All notions of 'nonviolence' within the Gandhian paradigm clearly come under the concepts of just struggle, resistance and defense, as do forms of violent resistance when taken up for liberation against oppression or violation. In spite of his assertions to the contrary Sharp's work, like that of others working in the Gandhian paradigm, remains a study of 'good' 'nonviolence,' in which only cases of struggle against oppression and injustice are examined. The Finnish 'case' is an excellent example: The original Russian nationalist 'attack' on the assertive Finnish nationalist mobilization can, from the

---

5 Steven Huxley, "Nonviolence misconceived? A critique of civilian-based defense," *Civilian-based Defense: News & Opinion*, vol. 7, no. 6, August 1992, pp. 3-5.

Russian point of view, be seen as a kind of resistance to Finnish threats to imperial security. In spite of the fact that for many years this 'resistance' included no physical violence those working in the Gandhian paradigm would never dream of calling it 'nonviolent action.' (p. 20)

The same point could be made about much oppression around the world today that is imposed through economic or social mechanisms. An example is the international economic system in which poor people in poor countries are impoverished through the operation of trade policies. Although large banks and multinational corporations operate almost entirely without direct violence, those using the concept of nonviolent action seldom refer to execution of policies that enrich the wealthy and exploit the poor as "nonviolent action."

The result is a lot of sloppy thinking among activists, who believe that certain kinds of actions are "nonviolent" when *they* use them but not when they are used by their opponents. It would make much more sense to be more precise about the term "nonviolent."

Johan Galtung tried to solve this problem by introducing the term "structural violence" to refer to oppression, exploitation and suffering caused by the routine operations of economic and political systems.[6] The Finnish resisters could be said to be acting against the structural violence of the Russian Empire.

The main problem with the expression "structural violence" is that it adds an enormous burden onto the term violence. Most people think of violence as direct physical violence. For much communication, terms such as exploitation and oppression may be clearer than "structural violence."

My friend Robert Burrowes, an experienced nonviolent activist and theorist, is unhappy with Huxley's use of the word "nonviolence." Robert argues that "nonviolence" should be used to refer to an entire world view: resistance to physical violence, resistance to structural violence, constructive work for a just society, and an appropriate personal lifestyle. This is in the tradition of

---

6 See, for example, Johan Galtung, *The True Worlds* (New York: Free Press, 1980).

Gandhi, who was opposed to all types of violence, whether physical, structural, cultural or psychological. From this perspective, actions by the Russian Empire shouldn't be included under the category of nonviolence.

My preference is to use the word "violence" to refer to physical violence and to use the expression "nonviolent action" to refer to action that is not physically violent. As much as I sympathise with Robert's commitment to the Gandhian meaning of "nonviolence," I think it will be a daunting task to communicate this meaning to wider audiences. As he suggests, it may be better to use the Indian word "satyagraha."

In 1969, a group of researchers asked over 1000 men in the United States about their attitudes to violence. Among the astounding findings were that over half thought that burning draft cards was violence and over half thought that police shooting looters was not violence. The researchers concluded that "American men tend to define acts of dissent as 'violence' when they perceived the dissenters as undesirable people."[7] Thus, it is common for judgements about whether something is good or bad to lead to it being seen as nonviolent or violent, respectively. In my view, like that of the researchers, this makes communication difficult. It is preferable that "violence" be used to refer to actions that hurt or destroy and "nonviolence" to actions that do not—whether we like the actions or not.

There is more involved here than just a choice of words. The important point is that particular types of actions should not *automatically* be considered to support a good cause. Nonviolent action may be helpful, desirable—some would say essential—for creation of a better world. But nonviolent action—in the sense of not causing direct physical harm—can also be used to maintain oppression and exploitation or to protect privilege.

This places a heavier burden on nonviolent activists than is usually recognised. They need to examine their goals as well as their methods.

---

7 Monica D. Blumenthal, Robert L. Kahn, Frank M. Andrews and Kendra B. Head, *Justifying Violence: Attitudes of American Men* (Ann Arbor: University of Michigan, 1972), p. 86.

For example, consider the many courageous campaigns of nonviolent action to protect forests. But do they protect an environment for the middle class at the expense of the interests of workers?[8] Are the actions of workers and forest industries considered to be nonviolent (ignoring the occasional violent outbursts)? What about the power of the state (backed ultimately by force), which sometimes is used against environmentalists but sometimes used to protect forests? I raise these questions simply to make the point that activists need to deal openly with difficult questions of right and wrong. Just because they use nonviolent methods does not automatically put them in the right.

Nonviolent action is not necessarily participatory

The Finnish resistance described itself as a national movement, defending a democratic political system against imperialist oppression. Actually, the Constitutionalists were drawn from the upper strata of Finnish society and were struggling to defend a society of limited participation. The institution of representative democracy, the Finnish Diet, had no representation from the masses at all. It was constituted out of four Estates: the Nobility, the Clergy, the Burghers and the Peasants. The Peasant Estate came from those owning land. Huxley notes that "In 1870 the Estates represented only about 1.5% of the population of over 1,750,000 people" (p. 83).

The Constitutionalists, in presenting their struggle as one supported by the rank and file, were on weak ground, and Russian officials knew it. Because of the need to build a wider base of support—and the Russian tactic of appealing to the Finnish masses—the struggle had a certain democratising impact. Even so, the basic approach of the Constitutionalists was to "educate" the masses in their national identity and the need for passive resistance to Russian impositions, rather than to democratise the institutions of Finnish society. In essence, the resistance was a defence of elite Finnish interests against imperial and elite Russian interests.

---

8 Useful insights on this are provided by Ian Watson, *Fighting over the Forests* (Sydney: Allen and Unwin, 1990).

This is quite different from a people's struggle, which is the usual picture imagined by today's nonviolent activists. The discrepancy should provide a warning to avoid misrepresentation of current struggles. It is common for leaders of both sides in a struggle to claim that they represent the interests and sentiments of the people. Huxley is critical of the commonly held view that "the action in which 'nonviolent' power is employed is somehow automatically democratic" (p. 23).

How much do most of us really know about the class structure of the intifada in Palestine, Solidarity in Poland or "people power" in the Philippines? In-depth studies of these and other struggles predictably reveal a complexity glossed over in usual accounts. We may still support these struggles. The point is that care should be taken in presenting a nonviolent struggle as one by the entire population.

In countries occupied by Nazi Germany during World War II, only a very tiny fraction of the population was active in resistance in the years before liberation was imminent.[9] Similarly, in most model conflicts using nonviolent action, leadership is provided by a small fraction of the people.

It is certainly true that nonviolent struggle offers greater *possibilities* for participation than military methods. All people can participate in nonviolent action regardless of gender, age and skills. But possibility is not always actuality. Activists need to be constantly aware of imbalances in participation and that their struggle may be serving the interests of a particular segment of society—and almost inevitably will be, given the social divisions within societies.

The struggle over ideas is crucial

Throughout the course of the Finnish struggle, the Constitutionalists waged a battle of ideas. They appealed to a mythical golden past of Finnish autonomy and democracy; they expounded on the injustice of the Russian initiatives; they challenged the

---

9 Werner Rings, *Life with the Enemy: Collaboration and Resistance in Hitler's Europe 1939-1945*, translated by J. Maxwell Brownjohn (London: Weidenfeld and Nicolson, 1982).

dominant Lutheran idea that people should give absolute obedience to government authority; they expounded the principles of passive resistance. All of this was a crucial part of the struggle.

Huxley: "It must be emphasized that noncooperation, disobedience and nonrecognition were the basic practical principles of passive resistance. But to be effective in practice they had to be combined with incessant moral warfare. In fact the manipulation of the moral and ideological environment is a central part of a great many conflicts throughout history" (p. 168).

Modern-day activists certainly pay attention to the struggle over ideas. Media releases, leaflets, articles and talks are standard parts of any group's repertoire. The planning of direct actions normally involves careful consideration of media coverage.

Yet, at the same time, most activists believe that their position would be widely accepted if only people *really* knew what was happening—if only they knew about the serious consequences of the destruction of rainforests or about the activities of repressive governments. Activists believe that justice is on their side.

Huxley's account suggests something more complicated. Justice is not something that exists in some pure form simply waiting to be recognised. Rather, people's very ideas about justice are the result of a struggle over ideas. The side that is able to "persuade"—with this "persuasion" involving both words and actions—most effectively is more likely to be the one that, in the aftermath of struggle, is seen to have justice on its side. Among Europeans, it used to be thought part of the order of things that kings ruled and that some humans were slaves. In the struggles to change these entrenched systems, both ideas and direct actions have been crucial.

The importance of ideas is shown by the intense discussions about which words to use to describe the struggle itself. During the Finnish resistance, the term "active resistance" referred to violent resistance. Then, as now, "passive resistance" suggested passivity, which was not what was intended. Huxley notes that, in order to overcome this, resisters "were forced to use clumsy phrases like 'passive active resistance,' which meant that resistance was to be carried out actively, but without violence" (pp. 174-175).

For the same reason, Gandhi took the initiative of trying to replace the term "passive resistance" with "nonviolent action."

The language of "nonviolent action" is certainly the one most widely used today.

One's use of language reflects one's political position. Huxley suggests that the language of the leaders of the Finnish resistance reflected their elite position and reluctance to mobilise the masses towards greater democracy: "maybe the Finnish Constitutionalists' retention of 'passive' and their zealous adherence to the upper class rhetoric of justice indicated their unwillingness to go beyond a certain border, not merely in relation to Russia but, perhaps more importantly, in relation to the Finnish people" (p. 175).

Huxley takes pains to point out how, in Europe in the 1800s, "passive resistance" had a fairly precise and recognised meaning. He notes that the term was replaced by "nonviolent action" for political reasons. As noted before, Huxley shows how "nonviolent action" is used by its proponents to refer only to actions that are considered "good." He is critical of the way that "nonviolent action" is used to describe events from different cultures and times with the assumption that a common dynamic is involved in each one. As he puts it, "It may also be deemed arbitrary and misleading to compare other so-called 'cases' of 'nonviolent' struggle to one another. Doubtlessly such comparisons may lead to an erroneous, or over-simplistic, association of historical events" (p. 18).

As much as I sympathise with Huxley's concerns here, I think that his challenge to the common use of "nonviolent action" is likely to fall on deaf ears. A more detailed and careful terminology, which Huxley would like to see, can be useful for historical studies, but serviceable language is also required for day-to-day struggles. Huxley could not be expected to provide an alternative vocabulary for this, since language grows out of use rather than external imposition. But, without any suggestions for how even to proceed towards developing a more precise and effective language for "nonviolent struggles," his critique lacks a positive dimension.

Conclusion

Constitutionalist Insurgency in Finland provides an opportunity to examine some of the conceptual underpinnings of the nonviolent "project":

• the assumption that selected historical examples provide an unambiguous message about a concept of "nonviolent action" that applies unchanged across cultures and eras;
• the assumption that those who use nonviolent action are necessarily on the side of justice;
• the assumption that nonviolent action is necessarily and inherently participatory;
• the assumption that if people just knew the truth, they would support the peace, environmental and other such movements.

If these assumptions are questioned, what are the implications for day-to-day action? Huxley does not address this, but it is something that activists would be unwise to ignore.

5
Lessons from the Fiji coups

On 14 May 1987, the Fiji government was ousted by a military coup led by Lieutenant Colonel Sitiveni Rabuka. The response to Rabuka's regime both within Fiji and overseas provides a useful test of the theory and practice of nonviolent action.

Fiji was taken over by the British as a colony in the 1870s. The native peoples are ethnically Melanesian. The British brought indentured servants from India to work on the sugar plantations. Today the so-called Indo-Fijians—born and bred in Fiji with ancestors from India—make up half the population of 700,000. Melanesians make up 45% and Europeans, part-Europeans and others the remainder.[1]

(In Fiji, the different ethnic groups are called Fijians, Indians and Europeans. However, most of the "Indians" long ago lost contact with India and are "Fijians" in the sense of being citizens. Therefore I prefer the clumsier terminology of Melanesian Fijians and Indo-Fijians, referring to both as Fijians, which does not confuse ethnicity with citizenship.)

The Europeans in Fiji long served their own interests by aligning themselves with the chiefs or aristocracy of the Melanesian Fijians. Fiji gained independence in 1970 under a constitution and

---

1 For background on Fiji see, for example, Brij V. Lal (ed.), *Politics in Fiji: Studies in Contemporary History* (Sydney: Allen and Unwin, 1986); Michael Taylor (ed.), *Fiji: Future Imperfect* (Sydney: Allen and Unwin, 1987).

electoral system designed around racial divisions. Melanesian Fijians were guaranteed ownership of most of the land, while members of parliament were selected in a complicated fashion in which each voter had four votes, for candidates of different ethnic backgrounds.

From independence until 1987, the Alliance Party held power under Prime Minister Ratu Sir Kamisese Mara. The Alliance was built around and supported by Melanesian Fijians. The opposition National Federation Party (NFP), which was built around and supported by Indo-Fijians, was riven by splits. In effect, ethnic divisions were exploited by the chiefs from Eastern Fiji, using the vehicle of the Alliance Party, to mobilise support for a feudal-style hierarchy that put them in a privileged position.

In 1985 the multi-racial Fiji Labour Party was formed. It was an attempt to promote class-based rather than race-based politics. The Labour Party criticised both other parties for serving the rich, and promoted the claims of workers, the unemployed and the poor.

The Labour Party rapidly gained strength and several NFP politicians defected to its ranks. In the 1987 election, the Labour Party joined with the NFP as a coalition and together they won control of parliament. It was this government that only six weeks later was toppled by a military coup.

Any military coup raises a range of questions. For example, who was behind it? Whose interests did it serve? What social structures or developments made it possible? What could have been done to forestall it or oppose it?

Here, my concern is with the potential for opposing coups and repression by nonviolent action. I begin by outlining some actions that can be taken against coups, especially by people in other countries. Then I compare this with the actions actually taken in relation to Fiji. The result is some lessons for future action.

The events in Fiji are complex. They have included apparent moves after 14 May 1987 toward civilian rule, a second coup on 25 September 1987, a repeat pattern of civilianisation—including introduction of a military-backed civilian government headed by Mara in December 1987—and the internal security decree of 16 June 1988 which established martial law. No attempt is made here to examine the politics of these and subsequent events.[2] I will refer mainly to the first coup and, in regard to overseas responses, refer mainly to responses in Australia.

Responses within Fiji

The coups in Fiji were almost entirely "bloodless." There was no organised violent resistance. This probably explains why there was relatively little violence by the Fiji military itself, at least compared to many of the military regimes in Latin America, Africa, Asia and Europe. Violent resistance tends to legitimise violence by the military as well as to unify it, while nonviolent methods tend to reduce violence by the other side. This at least is the claim by proponents of nonviolent methods, and it seems to have been borne out in the case of Fiji.

Nonviolent resistance within Fiji to the coups took a variety of forms.[3] At the most basic level, numerous people spoke out against Rabuka's regime, criticising its illegality and violations of human rights. Members of the Labour Party tried to build grassroots support, travelling to villages and explaining how the 1970 constitution guaranteed the rights of Melanesian Fijians. There were demonstrations and strikes in cities, and many shopkeepers closed their shops in protest. Even more powerfully, workers in the cane fields stopped work; the threat of failure of the sugar crop, Fiji's major export earner, was a serious one. Of long-term significance, many Fijians emigrated to escape the repressive political scene, and those leaving were mostly the educated and highly skilled.

The resistance to the Fiji military regime has been explicitly and consistently nonviolent. It is telling that the regime claimed that illicit arms shipments to Fiji, which were revealed by

---

2 See, for example, Kenneth Bain, *Treason at Ten: Fiji at the Crossroads* (London: Hodder and Stoughton, 1989); Satendra Prasad (ed.), *Coup and Crisis: Fiji—A Year Later* (Melbourne: Arena Publications, 1988); Robert T. Robertson and Akosita Tamanisau, *Fiji—Shattered Coups* (Sydney: Pluto Press, 1988); David Robie, *Blood on their Banner: Nationalist Struggles in the South Pacific* (London: Zed Books, 1989).
3 I have relied especially on the journal *Fiji Voice* (Fiji Independent News Service, PO Box 106, Roseville NSW 2069, Australia).

Australian Customs, were destined for coalition members, thereby trying to discredit them as planning violence.

The resistance in Fiji can be analysed readily in terms of the standard concepts of "nonviolent action." But these concepts do not provide a sufficient analysis of one vital part of the struggle: the struggle for allegiance at the level of ideas and cultural beliefs.

At first sight, this criticism of nonviolent action theory seems strange, since the whole theory is based on a struggle for allegiance. Nonviolent action includes an array of methods of direct communication and persuasion, all of which are designed to win over opponents or the uncommitted. Furthermore, one of the great advantages of nonviolent over violent methods is that they are less likely to alienate potential supporters. This account is fine as far as it goes. What it does not encompass, or includes only with difficulty, is aspects of the struggle for loyalty which involve aspects of culture and politics requiring an analysis of structures and belief systems.

The coups in Fiji succeeded with a minimum of force. There were relatively few soldiers involved. If there had been a concerted nonviolent resistance from the outset, it seems a good possibility that the initial coup could have been thwarted. But the reality was quite different from this hypothetical resistance. A large number of Melanesian Fijians supported the first coup while the Indo-Fijians failed to put up a show of support for the government. The mass rallies during the election campaign in support of the Labour Party failed to materialise in opposition to the coup.

The initial coup succeeded because it exploited ethnic divisions in Fiji, mobilising Melanesian Fijians and demoralising Indo-Fijians.[4] The use of ethnic divisions for political purposes has a long history in Fiji. The Labour Party itself represented a challenge to this political use of ethnicity, and the coup represented a reversion to this status quo.

Also involved in the early support for and acquiescence to the coup was the lack of vehement opposition by figures of powerful

---

4 It should be noted that many Melanesian Fijians opposed the coup and personally supported Indo-Fijians who came under attack. Fiji has never been as divided along racial lines as portrayed in many accounts of the coup.

symbolic importance. Mara, whose party had lost the election, did not exert his influence and reputation to oppose a coup when it was being sounded out just after the election, nor after it occurred. In the following weeks he appeared to serve Rabuka's purposes by being involved in the constitutional commission and the civilian governments that followed Rabuka. The Governor-General, Ratu Sir Penaia Ganilau, played a similarly ambiguous role. Other members of the council of chiefs also offered little resistance to the coup. All this made it appear to many that the formal justification for the coup—that the rights of Melanesian Fijians were threatened by the coalition government—had legitimacy.

The difficulty was not with nonviolent action itself, but rather with mobilising people to take the action. Without strong support from key symbolic figures, in the face of longstanding ethnic and other divisions, and lacking leadership, preparation and training in nonviolent action and strategy, a unified response was not made. This negative assessment should not obscure the considerable and powerful resistance that did occur. The point here is that most discussions of nonviolent action devote much more attention to the consequences of actions than to the structural and ideological obstacles to taking action in the first place.

Nonviolent resistance outside Fiji: the potential

The Fiji coups startled and disturbed many people in other countries. Outside Fiji, the stated reasons for the coups sounded hollow, and the ethnic divisions which helped sustain the new regime had little salience. What could people overseas do to support democracy in Fiji? Here I first outline a range of actions which might be taken by individuals and non-government groups, and then point to the ones which actually were taken up.

For a person in another country, it may at first glance seem difficult to intervene in events far away, but actually there are numerous ways to have an effect. (See the summary table on social offence, pages 64-65.) I have already discussed the vital importance for coup leaders to appear to be legitimate. This could be challenged by people openly criticising the new regime and demanding a return to the elected government. Given that Fiji newspapers, radio and television were censored immediately after the coup, the best available outlet for protesters in other countries was their own local media. Letters to newspapers, articles in magazines, programmes on radio, protest meetings and rallies all were effective in making more people aware of the situation. They also had an indirect effect within Fiji by affecting the opinion of people around the world and inhibiting the acceptance of the new regime by other governments.

Another way to support the resistance was to make direct contact. This includes letters to individuals, as long as censorship permits. (Censorship seems not to be have been too extensive after the Fiji coups.) Messages could be passed by visitors, whether tourists to Fiji or Fijians travelling overseas. There is also much routine communication for the purposes of commerce, navigation and weather analysis which could be used for passing political information. For example, computer communication carried out by banks or airlines could be used to transmit information. This could easily be hidden from casual observation by simple coding or putting it in channels designed for engineering checks.

Many other groups make contact between countries, such as diplomats, sporting teams and church officials. These contacts can be used to pass information and advice.

Even more direct is short-wave radio, which provides person-to-person communication over long distances. Because of its geographical dispersion, Fiji has a large number of short-wave receivers which could have been used for obtaining reliable information about the events. Significantly, the Rabuka regime tried to get people to turn in their short-wave sets.

Economic pressure is another potent tool, especially in the case of a small country like Fiji. Trade union bans on shipments to or from the country are one method. Another approach is the consumer boycott. In the case of Fiji, the major "good" most straightforward to boycott was the tourist trade, since tourism was Fiji's second largest export earner. Refusing to go to Fiji hurt the economy; writing a letter to a newspaper stating that one is refusing to go, and is taking one's tourist trade to more democratic countries, adds symbolic impact to this stand, and is effective even if one had not been planning a trip to Fiji.

Another approach was to provide direct support for nonviolent action within Fiji by offering advice and training. This could be done for Fijians travelling overseas, or done in Fiji by activists ostensibly entering as tourists. If a sufficient fraction of visitors to Fiji were actually nonviolent activists, the regime would be caught in a bind. Allowing the visitors to move unhindered would allow activists to build strength for the opposition, whereas security measures to monitor and arrest suspicious visitors would risk alienating genuine tourists and thus hurting the economy.

Finally, people overseas could provide refuge to refugees from the regime. Fleeing the regime does not by itself undermine its strength, but many refugees are able to become vocal once they are free from repression inside their home country. The availability of refuge also can encourage dissent from inside, when people know there are havens if necessary.

While all these measures are quite compatible and indeed predictable parts of social defence, in practice there has been little attention to the issue of acting against repression from an outside country. Most of the attention in the social defence literature is on nonviolent action within a country against foreign aggression, which is the normal "threat situation" for which military forces are traditionally justified. There is also considerable attention in this literature to opposition to military coups but, again, this opposition is usually assumed to be from within the country where the coup occurs. Yet for nearly everyone in the world, there are many more opportunities to take action against repression elsewhere than in one's own country. It is also much safer for the individual (though moral dilemmas can be severe, since one is intervening in someone else's society).

One reason why so little attention has been given to opposing repression in other countries is that the framework of states, including the United Nations and numerous treaties, places great emphasis on the evils of violating the territorial integrity and government prerogatives of other states. The great evil, at least as presented by governments, is attacking or subverting another state. Proponents of social defence may have imbibed this prohibition and thus neglected to consider nonviolent action which can offer a potent challenge to foreign governments.

I have purposefully not discussed action by foreign governments. In principle, they could play an enormously influential role in opposing coups and repression. In the case of Fiji, it would have been possible for governments of such countries as Australia and New Zealand to promote Commonwealth and United Nations sanctions, to hinder trade, to block tourists from travelling to Fiji, to cut off economic aid, to withdraw investment, to beam shortwave broadcasts encouraging resistance, and a host of other nonviolent actions. But, as I discuss later, governments are unreliable opponents of repression and, furthermore, their actions may be counterproductive.

Nonviolent resistance outside Fiji: the reality

There was no pre-existing organisation or network designed to respond to the initial Fiji coup. Therefore the actual responses outside Fiji were to a large degree improvised, just as they were inside Fiji.

The most obvious response in most countries was the mass media's publication and broadcast of numerous articles and reports about the coup. These varied in their analysis and their degree of condemnation of the coup. What is relevant here was the scarcity of information about how people could help oppose the coup. This partly reflects the lack of any authoritative body—of the stature of Amnesty International, for example—which could pronounce on appropriate responses. If such a body had existed, some of the news media undoubtedly would have reported its recommendations as news, even if not endorsing them.

While it is not surprising that the mass media provided little indication of how to oppose the military regime, more disappointing was the response in the "alternative media." In Australia, for example, two left-wing weekly newspapers, *Tribune* published by the Communist Party of Australia and *Direct Action* published by the Socialist Workers Party, published a large number of articles about the coup, all condemning it. But these articles gave remarkably little attention to how to go about opposing the regime. Aside from direct reportage of the events, continuing attention was devoted to the possible involvement of the United States Central Intelligence Agency in the initial coup. Yet whatever the role of the CIA, the early path of Rabuka's regime did not depend heavily on overt external military support. In any case, the presence or absence of CIA involvement would not have made a great deal of difference to practical action against the regime. The attention to the CIA seemed to reflect ideological antagonism to the US government and an attempt to fit the Fiji events into a standard Marxist analysis.

Another problem with the left-wing analysis of the coup was the assumption that capitalism was served by the events. Arguably, the coup, which devastated Fiji's economy, hurt both local and foreign capitalists. While class issues were certainly important, Marxist analysis elevated them above issues of local hierarchy (the chief system) and ethnicity.

Whatever its deficiencies, the left-wing press provided far more useful material to opponents of the regime than the mainstream press. *Tribune* and *Direct Action* offered background political analyses of Fiji and reported on opposition to the regime both within Fiji and overseas, all of which was highly useful to anyone considering their own role.

Among the Australian electronic media, the most valuable function was carried out by Radio Australia, which broadcasts throughout the South Pacific. Its straightforward reporting of the events could be received loud and clear in Fiji and provided an authoritative counterweight to the censored Fiji media. (The BBC World Service played a similar role.)

One of the major activities by opponents outside Fiji was organising public meetings, rallies, fund-raising and the like. Much of the initiative for this action came from Fijians living abroad. But while the media releases and public meetings of opponents helped to generate awareness and concern, apparently there was no overall strategy for promoting direct action.

One central activity was to lobby governments to take action against the illegal regime. This approach was supported by officials from the deposed Bavadra government and was eagerly adopted by many supporters overseas, who in turn hosted various visitors from the Bavadra government. Numerous letters were written and delegations organised to appeal to presidents, prime ministers and, not least, the Queen (the Queen of England—Fiji in 1987 was part of the British Commonwealth).

By my assessment, this approach was largely fruitless from the beginning. Governments are guided much less by legalities and justice than by pragmatic strategic assessments. The Fiji Labour

Party government promised a foreign policy more independent of the strategic interests of the United States and, for example, had a platform of banning visits by nuclear warships. Therefore it was easy to predict that the US government, while mouthing platitudes about democracy, would provide little support for opponents of the coup.

The Australian government, which has long been subservient to the US government when strategic military concerns are at stake, seemed bound to follow the US lead. Every ideological factor should have led the Australian Labor Party government to exert major pressure against the coup, remembering that the ALP had been thrown out of office in 1975 in a "constitutional coup" with some similarities to the Fiji events (but no military involvement).

As noted earlier, Australian government action against the coup could have been devastating. But effective nonviolent action was not taken. After a period of verbal condemnation and little effective action, the Australian government changed its practice of recognising foreign *governments* to one of recognising *states*. Thus it could recognise the Fiji state although it might supposedly disapprove of the new government. This semantic subterfuge served to obscure the double standards that would have been even more blatant had the new Fiji government been recognised while other military regimes remained in diplomatic opprobrium. Even so, the Australian government did not move to recognise the "states" of Afghanistan and Cambodia.

The large amounts of energy put towards lobbying governments, trying to obtain an audience with the Queen and so forth were a waste and a diversion. Governments are the least likely bodies to take action against the crimes of other governments, as shown for example by the abysmal record of governments in failing to act against genocide in other countries.

The statements and actions of governments are important, undoubtedly. The question for community-level activists is how to best use their energies to oppose a foreign military regime. Arguably, it is more effective to generate concern and action at the grassroots, which then will act as a pressure on governments as well. After all, governments are occasionally responsive to popular concerns. But without obvious grassroots support, lobbying has little hope of success if the lobbyists are not saying exactly what the government wants to hear.

Furthermore, government intervention could have done more harm than good. If warships and troops had been sent—as, according to later reports, was ordered by New Zealand Prime Minister David Lange but delayed and undermined by New Zealand military commanders—this could well have generated greater popular support for the Fiji regime and provoked greater levels of violence.

A much more effective channel for action against the Fiji regime was through trade unions. Bans on trade with Fiji were instituted by trade unions in Australia and New Zealand shortly after the coup, and these were a highly effective form of pressure.

The trade union bans were lifted after two months when it was claimed that trade unionists in Fiji were no longer being repressed. The struggle for loyalty within Fiji certainly encompassed trade unions, and both rewards and threats induced some Fijian trade unionists to reduce their opposition to the regime. This in turn allowed some foreign trade union officials to argue against the bans. They were encouraged in this by pressures from governments and corporations to leave the issue to "proper diplomatic channels." Bans were reimposed after the second coup in September 1987, and again lifted by top Australian trade union officials, in spite of rank-and-file support for their continuation, after dubious claims that Fijian trade union rights had been restored.

The story of trade union opposition has many complications, but the basic points are clear. The bans were a highly effective form of nonviolent action, as indicated by the amount of trade affected and by the Fiji regime's efforts to overturn them. But the maintenance of the bans depended on a struggle over the status and actions of the new regime as well as the degree of public support for trade union action. Once again the theory of nonviolent action gives a good account of the power of nonviolent methods but gives less direction on how to succeed in the struggle for legitimacy and so to maintain the action.

As mentioned before, tourism is a major economic activity in Fiji. After the coup, the number of tourists visiting Fiji dropped drastically: the country essentially received the wrong sort of publicity, and no longer appeared to be an idyllic haven, free of tension and strife. Tourism has suffered ever since, though it has been helped by cut-price tour packages and by various governments' tacit or overt acceptance of the new regime.

The overseas opponents of the coup could have, but did not, mount a major campaign around a boycott by tourists. For example, leaflets could have been distributed to all people visiting tourist agents, letters written to newspapers and a formal committee to promote "ethical tourism" could have made pronouncements against going to Fiji. (Some critics argue that virtually all tourism to Third World countries is part of the wider exploitative relationships between the rich and poor parts of the world, so whether it would be advisable to recommend any tourism as "ethical" is debatable.)

The advantage of a campaign around tourism is that it would affect, potentially, a large fraction of the population in countries such as Australia and New Zealand. Because holidays in Fiji are affordable by a sizeable proportion of people in these countries, the message that Fiji had become an undesirable destination would be a potent one. Tourists and potential tourists could also be encouraged to write to the Fiji government or Fiji Embassy saying that they planned to travel elsewhere until democracy was restored in Fiji. These actions are something that anyone can do. By contrast, government actions and even trade union bans involve only a limited number of people who make the key decisions; others can only lobby or promote discussion.

As mentioned, the tourism factor was potent even without concerted action to deter people from becoming tourists. With a plan of action mapped out in advance for such a situation, a tourist boycott could become a significant method of nonviolent action.

In summary, foreign government response to the Fiji coups was mainly rhetorical, and numerous governmental nonviolent actions which could have been made were not even mooted. The continuing efforts by overseas opponents of the coup to lobby governments had predictably poor results: most governments were much more interested in their immediate political and economic interests than in making stands for justice and democracy and in supporting grassroots opposition to the military regime. On the other hand, several other approaches were more effective. The large number of articles, letters and newsletters spread information; trade union bans were very potent economically and symbolically, while they lasted; and the tourism factor was important even though it was not pursued systematically.

Conclusion

The responses to the Fiji coups highlight an area which needs development: how to foster nonviolent action against forces of aggression and repression which are able to mobilise potent symbolic supports. Nonviolent action theory gives extensive guidance for taking action when it is clear to everyone who the aggressors are. It also explains why people decline to take action. But it is less helpful in showing how to mobilise people in an ambiguous situation in which the aggressor is able to use key symbols, such as ethnicity and nationalism, to nullify opposition.

The study of social defence normally focuses on opposition within the country in which repression occurs. Yet in many cases non-government opposition from other parts of the world can play a major role. The overseas opposition to the Fiji coups was vitally important. Yet there were no organisations with plans to confront such a situation. Advanced planning could include establishment of decision-making procedures, liaison with trade unions, plans for boycotts, networks involving a wide range of organisations, communications including short-wave radio, and regular training in nonviolent action. Since military coups regularly occur around the world, such planning (unfortunately) would not suffer for lack of events for application.

The Fiji coups stimulated some planning for similar threats in the South Pacific. The various Fiji support groups, the Nuclear-Free and Independent Pacific organisation and others are now in a position to take prompt and more organised action against repression elsewhere in the South Pacific.

One of the biggest problems facing activists is loss of interest in the topic by the public and the media. The outrage over the first Fiji coup kept the events in the news for quite a few months, and the second takeover by Rabuka in September 1987 rekindled interest. But the passing of time, the apparent legitimation of the regime through recognition by foreign governments, the dropping of trade union bans and the general difficulties associated with the lack of stimulating breakthroughs, made it very difficult to muster new initiatives against the regime. This was made all the more difficult by the various negotiations towards a new constitution and a civilian government, in which Mara and other established politicians participated. Outrage is difficult to mobilise against a regime that is cautious about appearing too overtly repressive.

Concern about opposing military repression should not be at the expense of general action and strategies for promoting justice and equality which, arguably, are what are required to help prevent the repression. It is almost always easier to prevent a coup than to reverse it. Indeed, preparations to oppose repression could possibly be more useful as a deterrent than as a treatment. The lessons from Fiji should be used to help prevent similar events elsewhere.

Finally, it is appropriate to note that the case for social defence in Fiji seems overwhelming. There is no obvious foreign military threat. The Fiji military forces number only a few thousands, so any moderate-sized force invading Fiji would receive little military resistance. As in many other countries, the major military danger to the Fiji people is from their own military, as events have clearly shown. A social defence system would not pose this danger, and so whatever its weaknesses would certainly provide more "security."

Social offence: taking the struggle to the aggressor

Rather than just planning for nonviolent resistance to an invader, there are also nonviolent ways to take the struggle to the opponent. Just as military defence always includes a capacity for offence, so social defence can include a capacity for offence. There are many possible techniques to oppose repression in other countries.

You can **Write letters.** This is simple but influential. Letters to repressive governments or their embassies in your country, stating your concerns, can have an impact, as demonstrated by Amnesty International's letter-writing campaigns against torture.

Letters to local newspapers are an effective way to get your message to the public. Letters to opponents of repressive regimes can provide valuable information and moral support.

You can **Organise discussions.** This can range from informal conversations between two people to large public meetings. Discussions and meetings are vital for sharing the information, insights and skills necessary to stimulate and organise effective action.

You can **Make public statements.** This can be done individually or as a group. You can produce and wear a T-shirt, pin up a poster, sign or sponsor a petition, make statements to the media and organise rallies.

You can **Support trade union actions.** This is of symbolic and economic importance. This action can be initiated or promoted by individuals in unions or by several unions as a group. Trade union bans and public statements have been very important in challenging military power in the Philippines.

You can **Support action through organisations.** Religious, sporting, artistic, women's, youth and many other groups can have an impact by distributing information to members, making public statements and instituting bans.

You can **Join boycotts.** Don't wait for governments to do it. Your shopping dollar makes a difference. Boycotts of South African goods have helped to end apartheid.

You can **Communicate through organisations.** Churches, diplomatic services, banks and other corporations often make regular contact across national boundaries, for example through phone calls and computer links. These channels can be used to pass other information in the course of normal business.

You can **Communicate via visitors.** Both personal and official visitors provide another means of getting information to and from a country.

You can **Refuse to be a tourist.** Instead, write to the foreign government saying you won't visit until democracy is restored. This was of symbolic and economic importance in the case of Fiji.

You can **Help people escape repression.** They need invitations, visas, money and jobs.

You can **Communicate via short-wave radio.** Repressive governments often cut off communications, especially just after a coup, such as in East Timor after 1975, in Poland in 1981 and in China in 1989. Short-wave radio allows people to communicate directly over long distances, outside government control.

You can **Join or support nonviolent interveners.** For example, the organisation Peace Brigades International sponsors nonviolent activists to enter violent conflict situations, such as in Guatemala and Sri Lanka. By their very presence, they inhibit violence. They may try to mediate between opposite sides, accompany individuals threatened by violence, organise publicity, or do practical work for the local community.

6
Nonviolence against hypocrisy in the Gulf

Following the Iraqi invasion of Kuwait in August 1990, the agenda for the peace movement was set by US President George Bush. That is something to worry about.

The Gulf crisis posed difficult questions for supporters of nonviolent action against aggression. How could nonviolent action have been used to stop Saddam Hussein? After all, he had been massacring his opponents for years.

The main focus in the Western peace movement was to support sanctions and to oppose the invasion of Iraq. The sanctions were not really nonviolent since they were backed by force.

There were some important nonviolent actions against war in the Gulf. Perhaps the most courageous was the Gulf Peace Camp, set up on the border between Iraq and Saudi Arabia by nonviolent activists from a range of countries.

Yet, it must be said, simply opposing the invasion of Iraq provided no answer to the question of how to use nonviolent action to challenge the occupation of Kuwait. Therefore, as well as supporting such nonviolent interventions, it is also important to look more broadly at the Gulf situation and draw lessons for the future development of nonviolent struggle.

Could nonviolent action have been used to stop Saddam Hussein's invasion of Kuwait? Hardly. Living in a vastly unequal and authoritarian society, the people of Kuwait could not have been expected to provide united nonviolent resistance against an invasion. What then is the role for social defence?

A clue comes from the massive hypocrisies involved in the US-led coalition against Iraq, in which Saddam Hussein was portrayed as the epitome of evil. Numerous governments proclaimed outrage at the invasion and occupation of Kuwait, yet they did nothing about the US invasions of Panama and Grenada. Nor had they taken much action against the Israeli occupation of Gaza and the West Bank. They did not intervene against the Indonesian invasion and occupation of East Timor nor against the invasion and occupation of Western Sahara by Morocco. Governments encouraged the sale of weapons to Iraq, in spite of Saddam Hussein's horrible human rights record. Most blatantly of all, they supported the Iraqi invasion of Iran with arms and intelligence.

These hypocrisies have been pointed out often, but one implication for the peace movement seldom has been noticed. The key point is that the agenda for the peace movement was set by those governments—especially the US government—that suddenly decreed that Saddam Hussein was the greatest danger in the world. Most of the media took their cues from their governments, and popular opinion was thereby shaped.

Although there are some two dozen wars around the world at any given time—such as, at the time of the invasion of Kuwait, those in El Salvador, Ethiopia, Angola, Afghanistan, Cambodia and the Philippines, many with massive loss of life—the US government declared that Iraq's invasion of Kuwait took precedence over all others. (Indeed, most of the other wars were ignored or forgotten by the world's major powers, in spite of their complicity in many of them.) The peace movement response did not challenge this view.

The result was that supporters of nonviolent action put themselves in the situation of having to provide solutions to a crisis created by state and military priorities. The crisis, by its origins and nature, made nonviolent intervention extremely difficult.

In retrospect, the key time to intervene nonviolently against Saddam Hussein was earlier in his rule, in the 1980s. The powerful 1980s peace movement, though, took little notice even of the Iraq-Iran war, preoccupied as it was with nuclear weapons. Another reason for the neglect of the Iraqi regime's excesses was the support given to it by a host of governments of all political persuasions.

This support took the form of diplomatic recognition, exports of weapons and other equipment, and turning a blind eye to brutality.

The agenda in the 1980s for the dominant powers was to tolerate or encourage Saddam Hussein. Most of the peace movement did nothing to challenge this agenda.

There were many things that could have been done in the 1980s to support the nonviolent opposition within Iraq, including publicity, boycotts, rallies, communication networks, peace camps and peace brigades. But aside from the regular efforts of groups such as Amnesty International, little was done in this regard.

The implication of this analysis is that nonviolent activists need to devote much more effort to set the agenda for nonviolent intervention. Rather than putting almost all effort into promoting social defence in one's own country or into intervening elsewhere according to government-dominated agendas, there should be much more energy directed towards developing networks and ongoing campaigns to support nonviolent struggles in other countries according to criteria and priorities set by nonviolent activists.

Part of any challenge to repression and aggression in other countries must involve a challenge to governments, especially their diplomatic support of brutal regimes and their exports of arms and technologies of repression. This challenge can be called nonviolence against hypocrisy.

Initially, such efforts may not do a lot to challenge the dominant agenda. But until promoters of nonviolent struggle do more to set the agenda, they will be continually asked to solve problems at the wrong time and the wrong place. How much better it would be to take the initiative and help to provide solutions to problems that governments prefer to ignore.

The Gulf crisis should not be considered a "hard case" to deal with by nonviolent action. It is actually a much harder case for the proponents of military strength, the arms trade and "pragmatic" power politics.

Instead of so many activists dropping their usual campaigns to protest against war in the Gulf, I like to imagine a peace movement confident enough to say "So what?" and to point out the hypocrisies and reaffirm its own long-term programme of action. Let's look to the day that the movement sets the agenda for governments, not vice versa.

7
Revolutionary social defence

Background

So far, no method of promoting social defence has had any notable successes. Only a few governments have shown interest in social defence, and none has taken major steps toward replacing its military forces by nonviolent popular resistance. (There have been inquiries in, for instance, Sweden, Denmark and the Netherlands, but with little continuing consequence.) Similarly, no community has trained itself in nonviolent resistance in a way that poses a comprehensive alternative to military defence. Given this lack of obvious successes, the discussion of prospects for social defence relies heavily on theoretical arguments, analogies and interpretation of historical struggles, most of which were not consciously linked to nonviolence.

Here I further examine the promotion of social defence, proceeding by looking at the problem of formulating a convincing scenario. My assessment is that no scenario has been presented which is persuasive both to advocates of elite reform and to advocates of grassroots initiative.

The main problem with the reformist approach, according to its critics, is that it does not deal with social structures, in particular with the vested interests in present military systems. It can be argued that most arrangements in society are based not on the logic of human needs (such as security) but on the interests of social groups in power, wealth and status. According to this view, the present military systems are in place because they serve the interests of national elites, military elites and corporate elites. Some government leaders may have the best of intentions to change the system, but they are unable to overcome powerful commitments to military systems that keep them in power. Any scenario, such as the social defence reform scenario, that ignores this issue is unrealistic.

This argument against social defence via convincing elites is very similar to the critique of disarmament negotiations. Analysts such as Johan Galtung and Alva Myrdal have argued that government disarmament negotiations are basically a facade, giving the illusion of possible progress while leaving the underlying war structures untroubled.[1] The same could easily apply to social defence negotiations, should things ever get that far. The advocates of the reform approach have not explained how they expect to avoid this fate.

The grassroots action approach to social defence suffers a different problem in terms of scenarios. There are many examples of dramatic popular nonviolent action which seem to hold the potential for a power equivalent to the military. But, according to critics, the results of such action are often pitifully weak or disastrously misguided.

For example, the Czechoslovak resistance to the 1968 Warsaw Pact invasion, although initially highly successful, was eventually crushed. Czechoslovakia became one of the more repressive Eastern bloc states for two decades afterwards.

The struggle for the independence of India, led by Gandhi, is one of the classic stories of nonviolent action. Yet some critics would say that India has not been decidedly less violent or a better place than many countries that obtained independence by other means. There was massive communal violence after the partition of India in 1947; the government of India developed nuclear weapons; the emergency of 1975-77 was a massive blot on the democratic process; the West Pakistan military assault on Bangladesh is one of the

---

1 Johan Galtung, "Why do disarmament negotiations fail?" *Gandhi Marg*, nos. 38-39, May-June 1982, pp. 298-307; Alva Myrdal, *The Game of Disarmament: How the United States and Russia Run the Arms Race* (New York: Pantheon, 1976).

century's major genocides; poverty, inequality and corruption remain extremely serious problems. Gandhi's positive programme, though supported by many resolute activists,[2] has made little headway in the face of Western-style development. Critics would conclude that the legacy of nonviolent struggle in India is not the most encouraging.

In the Philippines, the 1986 popular outpouring against the military regime of Ferdinand Marcos and in defence of Cory Aquino fulfilled one of the visions of the supporters of nonviolence: the triumph of nonviolent mass protest against threatened military attack. Yet the Aquino government was not a great improvement over Marcos: the war against "rebels" continued; landowners were defended against the poor; corruption persisted.

In each of these cases, the message concerning popular nonviolent struggle has been mixed. Nonviolent action seemed to be successful in the short-term, immediate struggle, but the subsequent history provides little indication of any permanent success. In none of these cases has nonviolent action become the standard means of struggle, nor has political development towards a nonviolent society ever seemed more than a distant prospect.

It is important to note that only in India was nonviolent action a conscious part of a long-term programme to change society. In the other cases, nonviolent action was used tactically and hence offered little prospect for institutional change.

The 1989 events in Eastern Europe involved far-reaching changes in political systems brought about, for the most part, without violence.[3] These events give great hope to the supporters of peace and freedom, but they do not fundamentally affect my argument. Although nonviolent struggle certainly played a crucial role in the Eastern European events, it was not waged against either a foreign military aggressor or a military government (except in Poland), the classic cases for evaluating the potential of nonviolent action for the purposes of social defence. In addition, further research is

---

2 Geoffrey Ostergaard, *Nonviolent Revolution in India* (New Delhi: Gandhi Peace Foundation, 1985).
3 For a useful analysis, see Michael Randle, *People Power: The Building of a New European Home* (Stroud: Hawthorn Press, 1991).

required to determine the exact role of nonviolent action in the political changes.

In most of the countries, the military did not intervene overtly to oppose democratisation. (The complex events in some countries, such as Romania and Yugoslavia, may qualify these comments.) Therefore these experiences cannot be cited as examples of nonviolent struggle succeeding, in a lasting fashion, against military opposition.

Most importantly, there have been no moves to eliminate the military in any of the Eastern European countries. In fact, the concept of social defence is far less known there than in the West. In Eastern Europe, nonviolent struggle was a key method used to bring down oppressive regimes, but nonviolent struggle has not been institutionalised in the new political-economic systems. Rather, most of the new governments have proceeded to rely on military forces in the usual way. (In a few cases, such as Lithuania and Slovenia, there has been strong official or unofficial interest in social defence.)

It may be that 1989 signalled the end of the Cold War, but that does not mean it has meant the end of the possibility of mass warfare, any more than 1815 signalled the permanent end of continental warfare in Europe. As welcome and significant as the 1989 events may be, they do not eliminate the problem of war. Therefore the issue of how to promote social defence remains a vital one.

In each of the examples above I have given only a brief sketch. It is not my aim to provide a political critique of nonviolent struggle. Rather, my point is that history so far has provided no clear-cut example of how a grassroots challenge to the military, leading to its replacement by social defence, might occur.

The rise of mass warfare

To provide the motivation for such a scenario, I turn to a different history: the rise of mass warfare and the modern state system. In this schematic history, my aim is not to provide political, economic or military detail, but rather to highlight some general changes in the nature of warfare which can be used to suggest the possibilities for social defence in the future. The key concepts here are participation, professionalisation and specialisation.

In feudal Europe, warfare was the preserve of a small minority. The bulk of the population, the peasantry, was rarely involved or indeed even affected by fighting. Soldiers were professionals, usually mercenaries.

The feudal relationship of warfare to society was connected to political and economic arrangements. Most economic production was for local use, and political power was decentralised (though quite unequal). There was no ready means of extracting economic surplus to support large standing armies. Hence the usual procedure was to raise a mercenary army for particular campaigns.

The feudal system was superseded by the modern state system. The military played a key role in this transformation, as it provided the basis for the gradual acquisition of greater power by the crown at the expense of the nobility. To support military expenditures, a larger portion of the economic product of the developing capitalist economies had to be extracted. To achieve this, tax collections and bureaucracies to handle them were required. The growth of the military and the state went hand in hand.

A key event in this process was the French Revolution, a revolution that strengthened the state and bureaucracy and incorporated mass support. The Revolution was seriously threatened by the surrounding traditional states and so, in order to avoid being crushed, it had to expand. This expansion took a populist, military form: the French revolutionary armies represented the first modern mass mobilisation of men for warfare.

The French revolutionary expansion in its turn triggered similar processes of state-building in neighbouring countries in order to defend against the French armies. This greatly accelerated the formation of modern states, with their political centralisation, bureaucracies for taxation and services, secret police, standing armies and centrally regulated economies.

The era of mass participation in warfare continued into the twentieth century, notably in the world wars. Large numbers of young fit men have been directly involved in armed forces. In the era of total warfare, other parts of the population have supported war efforts, especially through economic production; they have also been the targets of military attack, as in aerial bombing.

Mass participation has been associated with low professionalisation. Most soldiers in wars have been volunteers or conscripts.

Similarly, there has been a relatively low degree of specialisation. The rifle is a mass weapon, readily used by the ordinary soldier.

By contrast, in recent decades there has been a strong trend in industrialised countries towards low-participation, highly technological warfare. Modern weapons systems such as aircraft, submarines and guided missiles are exceedingly complex and require many more technicians and support personnel than frontline fighters. In the United States, one of the countries where this trend is most advanced, the army is largely made up of professionals, a large proportion of whom are technical specialists.

If the French Revolution symbolises the rise of mass participation in warfare, challenging the feudal pattern of small and temporary mercenary armies, then the nuclear arms race symbolises the return to warfare characterised by low participation, high professionalism and high specialisation. It is from this starting point that I turn to a scenario for the introduction of social defence, in analogy with the French revolutionary process.

Revolutionary social defence

A revolution can be defined as a rapid, basic transformation of key social structures in a society, such as the state and class structures, linked to mass revolts from below.[4] A military coup is not a revolution, since the channels for exercise of political and economic power are unchanged. On the other hand, the French, Russian, Chinese and Iranian revolutions, among others, changed the entire framework of economic relations, as well as the political leadership.

The phrase "revolutionary social defence" has two facets. It refers to the use of social defence in a potentially revolutionary situation, for example to defend a significant change in social relations. It also refers to the intrinsically revolutionary features of social defence itself: a replacement of the military by popular nonviolent action implies that the state can no longer rely on a

---

4 Theda Skocpol, *State and Social Revolutions: A Comparative Analysis of France, Russia, and China* (Cambridge: Cambridge University Press, 1979).

monopoly over the use of "legitimate" violence. Hence the survival of the state and of social institutions protected by the state, such as private property and bureaucratic privilege, is jeopardised. The introduction of social defence does not *require* a challenge to and replacement of major social institutions currently backed ultimately by violence, but this is certainly a possibility.

One possible scenario for revolutionary social defence involves the introduction of social defence in a revolutionary situation brought about for other reasons. For example, a radical party is elected to government, and is threatened by a military coup (perhaps supported by a foreign power). Organised nonviolent action to defend the government culminates in a conversion to social defence. Alternatively, nonviolent methods developed to resist an invasion are used to bring about radical changes in the society itself, including dissolution of the armed forces.

The introduction of full-scale social defence implies complete disarmament of the military. In the reform scenario, this disarmament is a carefully planned operation. In a revolutionary situation, it is far more likely to be people's disarmament, undertaken without sanction by government or military leaders, carried out to stop the use of weapons against the population. In order for such people's disarmament to succeed, it would have to be supported by significant portions of the military forces. It would involve disabling weapons systems, taking over military communication systems and dissolving or superseding military command structures.

The revolutionary changes brought about in this situation are most likely to be in the direction of radical democracy, namely the challenging of systems of unequal power and privilege associated with monopoly capitalism, state socialism, bureaucracy, patriarchy and the military itself. Whatever system is brought into being, it must have substantial popular support in order to be defended effectively by social defence.

So far I have assumed that people's disarmament and the introduction of social defence take place in a particular area: a country or substantial region. These developments, both the revolutionary changes and the introduction of social defence, will undoubtedly be perceived as threatening to other governments and militaries. Thus, as soon as social defence begins to be introduced in a revolutionary situation, it is likely to be threatened by external invasion or serious destabilising operations. It may be that "social defence in one country" is inherently infeasible or unstable, just like "socialism in one country." If the revolution does not expand, it is likely to be crushed or subverted from within by the supporters of military methods.

Instead of waiting to defend against an invasion, social offence could be initiated. In the case of revolutionary social defence, social offence means the active promotion of social defence in other parts of the world, especially where a threat to the revolution might arise.

A crucial aspect of social offence is communications, because the revolutionary society would almost certainly be slandered as corrupt and evil by its enemies, in order to justify attacks on it. Communicating the truth about methods and results would be essential.

The ultimate aim in social offence by the revolutionary society would be conversion to social defence in other parts of the world. If this failed, so might the revolution. But if it began to succeed, this could trigger a process of ever-expanding active disarmament, as "foreign threats" began to dissolve by people's actions.

In this process, there would undoubtedly be many bloody struggles and tragedies, as military and police forces were used to stamp out the revolutionary infection. Massacres might stop progress in some cases but they could also stimulate people's disarmament through the process of political jiu-jitsu associated with nonviolent action. It is even possible to imagine that some regimes might sponsor social defence themselves, in order to pre-empt revolutionary change.

Needless to say, this scenario is schematic. Any actual changes in this direction are likely to be long and drawn out, with surges and regressions over a period of decades. In the process, the results are likely to be far less than ideal. The "revolutionary societies" will no doubt turn out to be flawed in various ways; new forms of struggle, formally nonviolent but still manipulative, will develop to protect power and privilege; catastrophes and "excesses" will occur. Anything other than such an unstructured progression is wishful thinking. The reform vision of carefully planned conversion to social defence is certainly misleading, although that does not mean that chaos is desirable.

The analogy between the French Revolution and the scenario of revolutionary social defence should be clear. In both cases there is a dramatic increase in participation in social struggle, in armed struggle in the first case and in nonviolent struggle in the second case. (Social defence potentially involves a much *greater* mobilisation for struggle, since even those excluded from military service can participate.) In both cases the changes in participation in organised struggle are linked to revolutionary changes in social arrangements. In both cases, expansion of the revolution is the method of defending the revolution. In both cases, the original goals of the revolution may be lost, and new ways of exercising power may develop.

The aim in outlining the scenario of revolutionary social defence is not to foretell the future, but rather to stimulate thinking about strategies in the present. Revolutionary social defence is but one possible development, and as such is worthy of discussion and planning. Therefore, I now turn to the implications of this possibility for action today.

Some implications

1. The key to social defence may be its link with those social movements with the potential for promoting revolutionary change in social structure. Most important here are movements that pose a challenge or alternative to military and state power, especially movements for various forms of participatory democracy and workers' control. This category includes anarchist groups, the sarvodaya movement and portions of feminist, peace and environmental movements, and the green movement generally. None of these currently seems to have the potential to bring about change quickly, but appearances can be deceptive. The events in France in 1968 and in Eastern Europe in 1989 suggest the potentialities.

In practice, many social defence activists are also active in a range of social movements. The trouble is that social defence is commonly seen as something to do with unlikely invasions and coups, divorced from day-to-day social struggle. The challenge is to promote social defence in a way that integrates it with society and a broad perspective on security and development, rather than separating it off with a narrow orientation to invasions and coups.

Perhaps the initial step is simply to lay the groundwork for the rapid expansion of nonviolent action; when a suitable occasion arises, social learning can be extremely rapid. This can be aided if even a small number of committed individuals have prepared information sheets, tried out methods of organisation and decision-making, and organised communication channels.

2. In some circumstances, the survival of social defence may depend on the capacity and willingness for undertaking "social offence," the concerted use of nonviolent techniques to undermine potential aggressor regimes. This requires a somewhat different orientation than the usual idea of social defence, which is taken to imply preparing in one's own society to defend against attack from the outside.

Perhaps one reason why social offence has not been prominent in the studies of social defence is an association with military offence. In many circles, military offence is castigated but military defence is considered acceptable; the difficulties in separating these are glossed over. Another reason why social offence has been neglected is that it involves violating the "sovereignty" of another state; the invocation of sovereignty has long been a mainstay of governments and peace movements alike, despite inconsistencies in practice. In any case, social offence is much more interventionist than defensive social defence.

Social offence is not greatly different in form from much activity that goes on routinely. Telephone messages, radio broadcasts, visitors, diplomatic relations and commercial transactions are all standard ways of interacting between countries and between groups and individuals within them. Social offence simply puts a different content in the interactions. Like any other interaction, social offence is open to abuse, most obviously in the form of cultural imperialism. Nevertheless, it is based on action using nonviolent methods, which is quite different from military offence.

3. The introduction of social defence may be accompanied by extensive direct disarmament by popular action. This means disabling everything from guns and tanks to intercontinental ballistic missiles. It does not take much skill to remove bullets from guns or disable computers, but in some cases knowledge and care is required for direct disarmament.

The important point here is that almost no effort has been put into spreading knowledge and skills for direct disarmament. Numerous scientists and engineers have devoted their energies to constructing weapons, but few have developed simple ways for disabling and disposing of them.

The group most able to carry out direct disarmament is the military itself. This suggests that social defence advocates should make every effort to communicate with and organise within the military forces.

4. The promotion of social defence should not be the preserve of any particular group or orientation. Although I have presented here a scenario for the revolutionary adoption of social defence, it is not the only nor necessarily the most likely way that social defence will be implemented.

Furthermore, it is not clear how best to promote even the specific aim of revolutionary social defence. A strategy emphasising revolution may alienate some potential supporters and be partially counterproductive; on the other hand, such a strategy may provide such a threat to governments that they move in a measured way towards social defence. Conversely, the careful arguments for social defence by those favouring the reform path may, ironically, provide the best way to lay the groundwork for revolutionary social defence: the credibility of the careful scholars and lobbyists may actually serve better to spread the ideas of social defence.

These are simply cautionary comments. It is wise not to be overly committed to generalisations in this area, because no research has been done on the relative effectiveness of different methods of promoting social defence, nor are the criteria for evaluating different methods even spelled out, much less agreed upon. Because there has been so little experience in promoting social defence, and so little overt progress towards it, it is premature to rule out any method that seems compatible with social defence itself.

8
A tool for feminists?

Even a brief examination shows that the military is a mainstay of male domination. Military personnel are predominantly men, and the hostility of many soldiers to women is notorious. Women joining the armed forces commonly encounter discrimination, harassment and rape.[1] But there is more than this to the connection between patriarchy and the military.

The military is the ultimate defender of the institutions of the state and capitalism, which are key mechanisms for male domination. The existence of political and administrative hierarchies provides an avenue for implementing male-oriented policies, and of course the politicians and top-level bureaucrats who implement these policies are mostly men. Similarly, in the economic sphere, corporate hierarchies provide a channel for male advancement, male power and male-oriented policies. A key feature of this system is a highly competitive, career-oriented public sphere which is highly valued, largely separate from the nurturing private sphere which is not an official part of the economic system. Policies characteristic of this system include the "family wage," single-track career advancement, lack of child care and a privatised home life.

The military and the police are the two institutions officially licensed to use violence. This generally is done in defence of the state and the most powerful social groups. Any other use of

---

1 Cynthia Enloe, *Does Khaki Become You? The Militarisation of Women's Lives* (London: Pluto, 1983).

violence is officially considered criminal—except by men against women in their family, which is widely ignored, tolerated and, in many places, legal. This suggests the existence of a connection between patriarchy and the military at the level of a cultural acceptance of violence.

What strategies have a chance of undermining the mutually reinforcing systems of patriarchy and the military? Getting more women into the military is certainly *not* the answer. The connections between violence and masculinity are fundamental to patriarchy. More women in the military may help to reduce some of the worst exploitation of female soldiers, but it also will make those women subordinate to the masculine system of social control through violence. The liberal feminist solution of equal opportunity and equal representation of women in existing social institutions is doomed to failure. The military as a system must be challenged and abolished rather than joined.

For women to become guerrilla fighters is no better. In some liberation struggles, women have played an important combat role—though never have they approached an equal role at the top levels of command. In any case, those few guerrilla armies that have helped capture state power have been transformed, after "liberation," into orthodox military structures. The evidence shows that "national liberation" by armed struggle is not a promising road to liberation for women in the military nor, indeed, for those in civilian life.

Only the pressure of desperate struggle permits, *sometimes*, significant entry of women into combat roles. (The Israeli military is a good example here.) But when the pressure to survive is removed, women are quickly relegated to their usual subordinate positions.

The same applied to the prominent role of women in industry during World War II, when large numbers of men were in the armed forces. Women are allowed into men's jobs in times of necessity. Later, a roll-back to the status quo takes place.

Social defence, by contrast, provides a friendly framework both for an equal women's role and a feminist agenda—but only a social defence which is linked to challenges to the patriarchal structures of the state, capitalism and bureaucracy. In this model, women are empowered for nonviolent struggle in a nonhierarchical social system. They are empowered both to defend against aggression and to oppose male domination.[2] This is a scenario compatible with radical feminism and anarchist feminism.

Feminism and social defence

The fact that social defence allows participation by everyone is a dramatic contrast with military combat troops, which are composed almost entirely of young fit men. So in this simple sense of potential participation, social defence is much more egalitarian and, among other things, open to women.

(A complicating factor in this analysis is the declining role of front-line combat troops in warfare and the increasing importance of technology. Women are just as capable as men of servicing a jet fighter or pressing a button to launch a nuclear missile. Modern technological warfare could just as easily be carried out by women. The continued predominance of men in traditional occupations within the military shows that male power is the key, not any special strength or skill of men. For that matter, it would be straightforward to design rifles or tanks so that women could operate on the front lines as effectively as men.)

Empowering women against male violence. There is more to women's participation in social defence than equal opportunity. One of the radical elements of participation in nonviolent struggle against aggression is that it requires and develops skills which can be used in *other* struggles. For women, that means struggles against male violence and patriarchal institutions.

Some of the methods of nonviolent action useful in social defence include persuading opponents to change their behaviour, applying psychological pressure by embarrassment or social ostracism, and applying economic or political pressure through adverse publicity or boycotts. If these and other methods can be used against enemy soldiers or collaborators, they can also be used, today, against male behaviours that oppress women.

For example, the usual action taken against a known rapist is either (1) nothing at all or, occasionally, (2) a court case and

---

2 Pam McAllister (ed.), *Reweaving the Web of Life: Feminism and Nonviolence* (Philadelphia: New Society Publishers, 1982).

sometimes a gaol sentence. Given that prisons seldom rehabilitate individuals and commonly teach them crime, neither (1) nor (2) is satisfactory.

A group of women (and perhaps some men), experienced in nonviolent action, could choose from a wide array of methods to confront a rapist. They might go to him in a group and demand an apology. They might publicise the man's actions through graffiti, leaflets and letters. They might talk to the man's family, friends and work colleagues. They might boycott his business. They might recommend counselling by groups such as "Men Against Rape." (This approach may sound ineffectual. But I don't think so, especially after reading how women in an Indian community organised against a rapist.[3])

The besieged man might protest that he is innocent and demand a hearing in court, knowing full well that court cases involve trauma for women who testify and seldom lead to a just solution to the problem. The women might instead develop their own procedure for hearing the different sides to the story, a procedure that is sensitive to all concerned.

Courts are systems for maintaining the social order. They rest on the power of the state to arrest and imprison. A society without the military would have to have nonviolent systems for dealing with crimes. Since men are responsible for most crime in today's society, systems based on feminist methods of empowerment and nonviolent social control seem an obvious way to proceed.

Social defence is concerned with collective nonviolent struggle. It is, after all, proposed as an alternative to military defence. But many women are primarily concerned with the violence of individual men, sometimes strangers but more commonly husbands, lovers, fathers and friends. Social defence does not say what to do about sexual assault, beatings and harassment.

Feminism and social defence can gain from each other. A message from women's struggles against male violence is that policies for social defence need to be extended to deal with interpersonal violence. What social defence can provide in this connection is

---

3 Ila Pathak and Amina Amin, "How women dealt with a rapist," *Third World Resurgence*, no. 10, June 1991, pp. 39-40.

84   A tool for feminists?

skills and understanding of collective means of confronting violence.

Social offence for female emancipation. Feminists have many reasons to take up techniques of social offence to intervene in various parts of the world against oppression of women. There are many societies in which women are severely and systematically oppressed, for example by being sold into prostitution, forced to work long hours in dangerous factories, exploited and abused by husbands and male relatives, and subjected to genital mutilation.[4]

Women elsewhere can intervene against such practices by visits, publicity, boycotts, and a host of other techniques. Indeed, most of the methods of social offence against repressive regimes can be used against severe male oppression, and some new ones added.

One retort to such action is frequently heard: "we have no right to intervene in another society; we must respect other cultures." Intervention from white, wealthy countries seems uncomfortably like the old days of imperialism, colonialism and missionaries, all justified by "white men's burden" to save benighted natives from backwardness and sin. Are today's interventions really any different?

Respecting other cultures certainly is a good principle to keep in mind, but it should not override other more important principles, such as opposing exploitation, torture and killings. After all, some other "culture" might engage in ritual torture and execution. Few would tolerate such a cultural prerogative. Genocide is not acceptable just because it's happening within a single country. Intervention is justified in such cases.

The question then becomes, when does exploitation of women become serious enough to justify outside intervention? This is not easy to answer. There have been vigorous debates over female genital mutilation.[5] Opponents of Western intervention against the practice offer a number of arguments. They say that Western

---

4 Mary Daly, *Gyn/Ecology: The Metaethics of Radical Feminism* (Boston: Beacon Press, 1978); Maria Mies, *Patriarchy and Accumulation on a World Scale: Women in the International Division of Labour* (London: Zed Books, 1986).

5 See, for example, Alison T. Slack, "Female circumcision: a critical appraisal," *Human Rights Quarterly*, vol. 10, 1988, pp. 437-486.

intervention is a cultural imposition, that it may be counterproductive, and that it is more appropriate to act against Western women's deformations of their own bodies, such as through cosmetic surgery. Supporters of intervention cite the adverse health consequences of female genital mutilation and the lack of informed consent by the females, most of whom are children.

A heavy-handed approach—such as passing laws and prosecuting offenders—could well be counterproductive. A more effective approach is grassroots educational campaigns, relying as much as possible on local opponents of female genital mutilation. Such an approach is also more compatible with the principles of nonviolent action.

Direct action for women's liberation. Much of the public struggle for women's liberation has been to change oppressive laws and policies. For example, the struggle for reproductive rights—including the choice of different methods of contraception, and abortion—has been waged through courts and legislatures. The keys to ensuring women's reproductive choices are seen as supportive laws and policies.

Ironically, this means relying on male-dominated institutions: the medical profession, politicians, government bureaucracies. Women are placed in the position of being clients, petitioners and lobbyists. Their own skills in taking action directly are left undeveloped.

Another approach is for women to develop and practise the skills to control reproduction. Women's health groups have shown that women who are not physicians are quite capable of carrying out safe abortions. Women might decide to develop networks for production and distribution of the "abortion pill" RU-486. In other words, women should be ready to take direct action to control their fertility, rather than relying entirely on laws and policies.[6] Such a strategy is quite in keeping with the "alternative institutions" strand of nonviolent action.

---

6 Liz A. Highleyman, "Reproductive freedom in everyday life," *Love & Rage*, vol. 3, no. 2, February 1992, p. 6; Lisa Loving, "The abortion underground," *Kick It Over*, #29, Summer 1992, pp. 15-18; Julius A. Roth, "A sour note on *Roe* vs. *Wade*," *Research in the Sociology of Health Care*, vol. 9, 1991, pp. 3-8.

It is impossible, in this context, to avoid mentioning the struggles over abortion, including major confrontations at abortion clinics, especially in the United States. Many opponents of abortion consider it to be murder and believe that extreme means are justified to stop it. Proponents of having a choice of abortion do not see it as murder. They believe that a foetus is not yet a human or not yet a "life worth living."

The conflict is complicated by connections with other attitudes and stands. A large fraction of opponents of abortion fully support military preparedness and wars, and also oppose measures such as sex education and free contraceptives which, arguably, would reduce the demand for abortion. Antiwar activists are more likely to support the availability of abortion, and refer to the oppression of women and the blighted lives of children that are associated with lack of reproductive choice. There are a few groups which combine an antiwar and antiabortion stance.

The periodical *The Nuclear Resister* is produced to document and support those who have been arrested for opposing nuclear power and nuclear weapons. In one issue the editors included annual figures for those arrested for opposing abortion—a figure greater than all nuclear-related arrests—for the purpose of comparison, not advocacy. This caused an outpouring of passionate letters, some criticising the editors for even mentioning antiabortionists in the same context as antinuclear activists, others pointing to the covert use of violent methods by antiabortionists.[7]

It is certainly true that both sides in the dispute primarily use nonviolent methods.[8] But both sides also look to the state as an actual or potential ally in their cause. They would like to have the law on their side and have the police arrest and, if necessary, imprison those who resist laws supporting their own position.

---

7 *The Nuclear Resister* (PO Box 43383, Tucson AZ 85733, USA), no. 60, 15 February 1989, p. 2 and no. 61/62, 2 May 1989, pp. 2-3, 12-13.
8 Victoria Johnson, in an unpublished paper, argues that the approach used by Operation Rescue systematically differs from both principled and pragmatic nonviolence, and calls it "quasi-nonviolence." She can be contacted at the Department of Sociology, University of California, Davis CA 95616, USA.

In a society without formal violent sanctions, the struggle over abortion would be waged almost entirely with nonviolent methods. It could still be vehement! I don't know how the struggle would be resolved. I'd like to imagine that abortion could be minimised while women gained maximum control over their own lives, including sexual activity and reproduction. Or, perhaps, different communities would arrive at different decisions; those strongly disagreeing would be free to move away.

Could social defence be patriarchal? In theory, a strong system of social defence would mean that women were trained in skills of nonviolent action and, therefore, that these skills could be used in struggles to liberate women from male oppression. But practice is often quite different from theory. Capitalism, representative democracy and state socialism are each gender-neutral—in theory. In practice, these systems have been patriarchal: dominated by men and operating to oppress women. Why should social defence be any different?

It is quite possible to imagine a social defence system in which:

• most of the key planners and decision-makers are men;

• there are experts who are crucial to the resistance, such as skilled factory workers, computer programmers and gifted communicators, most of whom are men;

• most of those on the "front line" in confrontations are men, while most women stay at home with the children.

With government-implemented social defence, Sharp-style, this pattern would be inevitable: one male-dominated defence establishment would be replaced by another. But it's also possible with a grassroots approach to social defence. After all, many anti-establishment groups are just as patriarchal as the organisations they hope to replace.

All this points to a simple conclusion. Social defence groups must incorporate a feminist agenda and social defence should be taken up by feminist groups. Although this is a "simple conclusion," doing it in practice is an enormous challenge.

"**Surely you wouldn't just sit and do nothing while soldiers raped your mother or your wife?**" Questions such as this are often tossed at supporters of nonviolence.

Response 1. I would do my best to use nonviolent methods to prevent and stop rape. Using violence might make the situation worse (see John H. Yoder, *What Would You Do?*, Scottdale, Pennsylvania: Herald Press, 1983).

Response 2. That isn't the real issue. Social defence is about the collective defence of a society, and whether nonviolence is a better way to do this.

Response 3. Military systems are a major contributor to rape, not a solution. Armies are commonly involved in rape of civilians as well as killing and looting. Many female soldiers and wives are raped in "peacetime." Anything that helps to remove or replace military systems also helps to reduce rape.

Response 4. Most rapes in our society are by people known to the woman—especially husbands. There is also a much higher rate of child sexual abuse—by male relatives, especially fathers—than most people realise. Scare-mongering about rape by strangers, including enemy soldiers, diverts attention from the most important issue, male domination. Armies are male dominated, and can only contribute to the problem.

Response 5. Almost all combat soldiers are men, and armies are masculine institutions. Associated with this, women are often expected to be passive and are not encouraged to develop their skills at resistance.

Social defence challenges this pattern. It involves both men and women developing skills for nonviolent struggle. Many of the things involved in developing social defence—including developing support networks, nonviolent action skills and individual and community self-reliance—can also be used to act against rape.

It is a challenge for us to develop campaigns against rape that are linked with campaigns towards social defence. There are some positive connections, unlike the situation with military defence.

Response 6. If there's a military coup, what are *you* going to do to stop rape by soldiers—especially when they threaten to shoot the woman if you resist?

9
What about the police?

Let's suppose that the military has been abolished and social defence has been introduced. Would there still be police? Would they be armed? If so, couldn't they become an oppressive, military-like body? If not, how would unarmed people control crazy people with dangerous weapons?

These are difficult questions. Social defence writers have avoided them.

The first thing to point out is that there are great similarities and strong connections between the military and the police. They are the only two agencies of the state which are considered to have a "legitimate" right to use violence. So, in terms of social structure, the military and the police are complementary. They are two sides of the same coin: organised violence in support of the state.

This becomes obvious in a few circumstances. The police are regularly used to control internal unrest: to take action against "unruly" protesters, strikers and radical political groups. They engage in surveillance, disruption, harassment and beatings of political dissidents who might threaten the status quo. But sometimes the police are not strong enough for this. Then the military is brought in to break a major strike or to spy on political radicals.

On the other hand, the police sometimes start taking over the techniques of the military. They acquire powerful weapons for "crowd control," surveillance and even torture, and are trained in methods of attack and defence that are typical of an army. This is the militarisation of the police.

The similarities are many:

- surveillance using taps, bugs and spies, in order to acquire knowledge of "the enemy";
- training in methods of dealing with collective violence (or simply "collective action") by "the enemy";
- prisons or prison camps for those who are captured;
- sharing of knowledge, trade in weapons and exchange of personnel between different allies (police forces in different regions or countries; militaries in allied states);
- an abiding interest in social control, usually to maintain the power of the existing government but always to ensure the existence of some sort of central government and the necessity for the police and military themselves.

My conclusion is simple. Getting rid of the military is not enough. It is also necessary to get rid of armed police forces.

This analysis applies also to the "political police," otherwise known as secret police, spy agencies and "intelligence services."[1] Whatever the name, they should be abolished.

Costa Rica is a country without an army—it was abolished in 1948. But police forces have been maintained and been used against labour and peasant revolts. For Costa Rica, getting rid of the army was only partial demilitarisation.[2]

Peace activists are acutely aware of the worldwide trade in arms. There is also a worldwide trade in the "technology of repression," namely all the equipment and weapons used by police forces and militaries to repress opponents of the state. This includes surveillance equipment, riot-control weapons and implements for torture. The biggest exporters are familiar names: the United States, Russia, Britain, France, Germany, Italy.[3]

---

1 Thomas Plate and Andrea Darvi, *Secret Police: The Inside Story of a Network of Terror* (London: Abacus, Sphere, 1983).
2 Tord Høivik and Solveig Aas, "Demilitarization in Costa Rica: a farewell to arms?" in Andreas Maislinger (ed.), *Costa Rica: Politik, Gesellschaft und Kultur eines Staates mit ständiger aktiver und unbewaffneter Neutralität* (Innsbruck: Inn-Verlag, 1986), pp. 344-375.
3 Steve Wright, "The new technologies of political repression: a new case for arms control?" *Philosophy and Social Action*, vol. 17, nos. 3-4, July-December 1991, pp. 31-62.

Towards nonviolent policing

If the defence system is to rely solely on nonviolent action, then the police force, to be compatible, should also rely solely on nonviolent action.

Now, some people will say, "Why have police at all? They are inevitably oppressive." My view is that any society, even one relying entirely on nonviolent action, must have methods for social control. Even without tanks and guns, there is great scope for undesirable action: murder, child abuse, exploitation, even savagery. For whatever reason, some people will sometimes do such horrible things that others will feel obliged to stop them.

A society in which anyone can do anything they want is impossible. It's not a question of social control or no social control, but rather a question of what sort of social control. Who makes the decisions, who implements them and how? It may be that the word "police" is inappropriate, but the process of *policing* is necessary.

Military defence is said to be a way of defending against external aggression, but it's also a way of maintaining order in society. The same can be said of social defence. The idea of nonviolent policing makes explicit and gives legitimacy to nonviolent action's potential for maintaining order in society.

An unarmed police force is certainly possible. After all, it's what Britain used to have, and many local communities still have. (Indeed, Britain's police are still supposed to be unarmed, but a process of militarisation has long been under way.)

But although a nonviolent police force is possible,[4] it is not necessarily easy to move from armed to nonviolent police, especially when the trends are running the other direction. Indeed, it is exactly like the difficult problem of moving from armed to nonviolent defence. In my view, the same principles apply: the change must come from the grassroots and be based on nonviolence. General strategies include:

---

4 There is a distinction between nonviolent and unarmed. "Nonviolent" implies using no violence by choice, whereas "unarmed" implies arms are simply not available but might be used if they were. For example, the *intifada* in Palestine is primarily an unarmed uprising, not a nonviolent one, a point nicely made by Andrew Rigby in *Living the Intifada* (London: Zed Books, 1991).

- exposing and challenging abuses by police forces;
- developing and using community-based methods for maintaining social order, including mediation and conflict resolution techniques, nonviolent patrols[5] and community-based justice systems;
- formulating plans for conversion of police personnel, skills and facilities to nonviolent alternatives;
- pursuing programmes for social justice which eliminate many of the incentives for crime.[6]

Finally, is it really a good idea to have a separate *police force*, even if it is nonviolent? This might not be necessary if nearly everyone learned techniques of nonviolent action. There is a wealth of information on how to do this,[7] much of which can be applied to "policing." Certainly, the more people who are skilled in nonviolent action, the smaller the danger that any formal nonviolent police can misuse their positions of responsibility.

What about prisons?

Conventional prisons, which lock criminals away with little prospect of rehabilitation, are symbolic of the repressive power of the state. Locking up a person is a form of violence. Would there be such prisons in a society relying on nonviolent action for social control?

Before addressing this question, let me first respond to the fear that prisons are essential to prevent a massive crime wave. First, it is well documented that prisons actually promote criminality: people locked away are more likely to learn the ways of crime than be encouraged to give them up.

---

5 A useful discussion is Edward Elhauge, "San Francisco's Queer Street Patrol," *Ideas & Action*, #16 [1992], pp. 24-30.
6 Elliott Currie, *Confronting Crime: An American Challenge* (New York: Pantheon, 1985).
7 See, for example, Virginia Coover, Ellen Deacon, Charles Esser and Christopher Moore, *Resource Manual for a Living Revolution* (Philadelphia: New Society Publishers, 1981); Martin Jelfs, *Manual for Action* (London: Action Resources Group, 1982). The most important sources of information are skilled nonviolence teachers. They have many skills that cannot be explained in writing.

Second, a large fraction of prisoners pose no danger to society. Drug users and drug sellers are not really dangerous in themselves, but are a product of the illegality of certain drugs. Many murders and assaults occur within the family; the individuals responsible usually pose no particular danger to people outside that family. Then there are the large number of people in prison basically because they are poor, uneducated or stigmatised because of race. They may be arrested because of vagrancy, drunkenness or petty stealing, or simply be harassed or provoked by police. Prison becomes a repository for the outcasts of society. Prison is the least suitable way to respond to this problem with society.

If such groups were kept out of prison, there would be a mere fraction remaining. This is completely clear when imprisonment rates in different countries are compared. The fraction of the population imprisoned in the United States is ten times greater than, for example, in Ireland. People in Ireland are in no more danger from berserk criminals who should be in prison than are people in the US. Indeed, quite the contrary, since US laws and police policies help create the very problem they are supposed to control.

The police probably cause more crime than they prevent. Criminologists know that the crime rate has little connection with the level of policing or imprisonment. Most prisons breed crime, and most police forces breed corruption.

If everyone in prison were released in the next few years, it would make very little difference to the level of crime in a community. It is salutary to remember that most crime is never punished, because the crimes are either legal or carried out by groups that are not brought to justice. This includes regular and severe beatings of prisoners by police and prison warders, production and sale of legal drugs such as cigarettes, recruitment of ex-Nazis and other murderers by spy agencies, sales to Third World countries of dangerous goods that are banned in their country of production, and fraud and embezzlement by corporate executives.

Most of the world's governments have supported the most repressive of rulers, including mass killers. The list includes the Indonesian military regime, which came to power with the killing of perhaps half a million people, and the Khmer Rouge in Cambodia, who were responsible for political murders of perhaps a million of their own people. What is the point of putting local thieves in prison if mass murderers are wined and dined? Social control, of course. It all goes to show that it is not those in prison who are the main danger!

Most of all, the military system is itself a criminal operation. After all, what is war except organised crime controlled by governments? In the words of sociologist Charles Tilly, "If protection rackets represent organized crime at its smoothest, then war making and state making—quintessential protection rackets with the advantage of legitimacy—qualify as our largest examples of organized crime."[8]

Now, to return to the question that I postponed answering earlier: "Would there be such prisons in a society relying on nonviolent action for social control?" My answer is "certainly not!"

Thomas Mathiesen has examined the evidence and concluded that prisons don't work: they don't rehabilitate, they don't prevent crime and they don't provide justice.[9] He argues that prisons should be phased out and abolished.

But how can a society without prisons be brought about? It won't be easy! Mathiesen says that a massive information campaign is essential to counter the ideology of prisons, plus initiatives from a socialist government to phase out prisons. I agree with the information campaign, but suspect that few governments, socialist or otherwise, will be willing to forego the prison as a means of social control. A more grassroots-based approach would include:

• moves towards a more just and egalitarian community, in order to remove poverty, racism and exploitation, which are common causes of some types of crime;

• challenges to patriarchy, in order to reduce male violence;

• moves for nonviolent policing, in order to reduce crimes committed by police;

---

8 Charles Tilly, "War making and state making as organized crime," in Peter B. Evans, Dietrich Rueschemeyer and Theda Skocpol (eds.), *Bringing the State Back In* (Cambridge: Cambridge University Press, 1985), pp. 169-191.
9 Thomas Mathiesen, *Prison on Trial: A Critical Assessment* (London: Sage, 1990).

• struggles by prisoners and their supporters, in order to stop crimes against prisoners and reduce the function of prisons as "schools in crime";
• social defence, in order to build skills in nonviolent action and help defend the social struggles listed here.

10
Social defence and the environment

Organising a community for the most effective nonviolent resistance to aggression actually leads to an impressive environmental policy. But before discussing this, it is useful to outline some of the connections between war and the environment and between the environmental and peace movements.

War and the environment

War is normally thought of as a violent struggle whose main victims are people. But the environment is also a prime victim.[1] The ancient Romans, after defeating Carthage, prevented its resurgence by putting salt on its fields to prevent the growing of crops. The Indochina war involved a full-scale attack on the environment by US technology, with conventional bombs saturating the countryside and napalm stripping leaves from trees. The torching of hundreds of Kuwaiti oil wells was a spectacular consequence of the Gulf war. Nuclear war would have catastrophic effects on the environment through blast, heat, radiation, fires and nuclear winter.

In case this isn't enough, military planners have conceived many "environmental weapons" such as triggering earthquakes and tidal

---

1 Stockholm International Peace Research Institute [Arthur H. Westing], *Warfare in a Fragile World: Military Impact on the Human Environment* (London: Taylor & Francis, 1980).

Social defence and the environment 97

waves. Also waiting in the wings are biological weapons, which could have enormous effects on plants and animals.

Even without war, the military establishments of the world have a major impact on the environment. After all, they take up a significant proportion of the world's economic production, energy use and so forth. Moreover, much of what military forces do involves destruction rather than production: shells are routinely fired against practice landscapes and the occasional nuclear vessel sinks to the bottom of the ocean.

Another connection between military systems and the environment comes through the military imperatives behind certain "commercial" technologies. Nuclear power is the classic case. Nuclear rather than solar power was favoured in part because of military connections. Nuclear research could lead to military applications as well as power production; uranium enrichment plants and nuclear power plants could be used for joint military and civilian purposes (though the anti-nuclear power movement has succeeded in stopping most military use of spent fuel from civilian nuclear power plants); nuclear scientists and engineers who made a name in the nuclear weapons business could continue their careers with nuclear power. Therefore, some of the responsibility for nuclear disasters such as Chernobyl can be attributed to the military. Of course, military nuclear disasters are horrifying enough, especially the 1957 incident at Chelyabinst in the Soviet Union. Furthermore, these are nothing compared to what was—and still is—the likely environmental impact of nuclear war.

These connections between military and civilian nuclear developments are replicated in the areas of chemical and biological weapons. The military continues to be a prime influence in scientific research and technological development. Sometimes the environmental consequence of this is not so great, as in the case of computing. In other cases, such as genetic engineering, the potential for environmental destruction is vast.

A final and fundamental connection between the military and the environment lies in the maintenance of inequality in an industrial society. A great deal of the responsibility for environmental destruction can be attributed to policies which serve the interests of the rich and powerful minority in industrialised societies. This includes the automobile industry, the oil industry, the chemical industry, the forest industry, and so forth. The rich and powerful shareholders, executives and managers gain the most from these industries. They would not gain so much from a different pattern of development: cities designed around walking and bicycling, reuse of products (rather than new production or even recycling), production for basic needs rather than creation of new wants, and priority given to satisfying work rather than money to buy consumer products.

This is all very well, but what's the connection with the military? Quite simply, the industrial system based on unequal privilege and power can continue only because the military—and the police—are there to smash challenges to it. In industrialised societies, such as the United States and Western Europe, there is seldom a need these days for the military to be brought in against workers or the community. The processes of persuasion through schooling and the media, the legitimacy of electoral politics, plus the cooption of the middle classes through consumerism, serve to maintain the social order without much overt violence. But in other parts of the world, there are fundamental challenges to the system of organised inequality through industrial capitalism, including radical political parties and people's movements.

To be sure, some of these alternatives are based on just as much inequality as industrial capitalism. But they do offer a challenge to First World exploitation of Third World economies, usually justified as part of the process of economic "development." Minerals must be available for extracting, forests for cutting, rivers for damming, and fields for monocultures using artificial fertilisers and pesticides. If the local people resist such activities, then out comes the military to maintain a form of "development" that has enormous impacts on the environment.

The environmental and peace movements

Since there are so many connections between the military system and environmental destruction, it is appropriate that there are strong links between environmental and peace movements. The nuclear issue illustrates the connections. In the late 1950s, concern about nuclear weapons became a major social issue, with a special emphasis on fallout. This concern faded in the early 1960s, to be replaced by the growing anti-Vietnam war movement. Meanwhile, the environmental movement came of age in the 1970s. With the peace movement moribund, anti-nuclear power activists kept attention on nuclear war through their concern about nuclear proliferation. Then in the 1980s there was a massive resurgence of concern about nuclear weapons. In the 1990s, attention to environmental issues has expanded while the peace movement has faded away.

So, to some extent, each movement has kept the issues of the other alive, on the agenda, when the other is in a low period. Of course, there are frictions about priorities too. But the tendency is towards cooperation, especially with the increasing emphasis on green thinking and politics.

From the point of view of social defence, a second and crucial connection between the environment and peace movements is the use of nonviolent action. The use of nonviolent action as a deliberate choice, for reasons of both principle and tactics, is increasingly frequent.

This may seem an obvious choice for many peace activists, since they are trying to develop an alternative to war: they have used vigils, fasts, marches, rallies, occupations and camps to challenge wars, shipments of weapons and military bases. Yet nonviolent action seems just as much a feature of environmental activism, with a similar array of methods used against nuclear power, forestry operations and chemical plants.

An awareness and experience of the dynamics of nonviolent action is perhaps the most important factor affecting whether a person supports social defence. The increasing sophistication of environmental nonviolent action is creating a group of people who would readily join a social defence movement—should such a movement ever get off the ground.

A community even partially organised for social defence would have a great capacity for resisting assaults on the environment. Since a much wider fraction of the population would be alert to the possibilities for direct action, companies or governments undertaking environmentally damaging activities would have more employees aware of how to offer resistance. They could provide information to resisters in the field, could directly subvert equipment or plans within the organisation, or could organise strikes or work-to-rule campaigns.

Environmental implications of social defence policy

Developing a "social defence policy for the environment" is simply a matter of spelling out general policies for a society to be most able to nonviolently resist aggression and then noting the implications for the environment. Here are some examples.

Energy. Dependence on central energy supplies, such as oil for vehicles or electricity for dwellings, makes a community vulnerable to attack.[2] The alternative is energy efficiency and use of local energy supplies. Solar design of dwellings, for example, means that people will not freeze in winter even if outside energy supplies are cut off.

Using local energy supplies means that an aggressor cannot coerce an entire population by capturing a few strategic points of energy production or distribution. To provide energy self-reliance, local energy supplies would not necessarily be environmentally sound. They could be coal, gas, solar or wind. In practice, local energy self-reliance is much more likely to be based on renewable energy, because deposits of fossil fuels are concentrated in a few locations. Not many suburbs have a coal mine!

It might make sense for communities to have stores of fossil fuels in case of emergency. But stores have a finite lifetime, whereas renewable energy usually lasts longer. (Biofuels such as trees take a while to grow.)

Industry. One obvious target for an aggressor is large-scale industry, such as steel production, automobile production, oil refineries and chemical plants. The production could be diverted to serve the aggressor, or shut down to apply pressure to the community.

Therefore, a community planning for social defence would be wise to replace large-scale industry. There are several options. One is to introduce local small-scale production to produce the same thing. For example, an integrated steel plant can be replaced by numerous minimills in different locations. Minimills rely on local scrap and are much more able to vary the amount of steel produced.

---

2 Amory B. Lovins and L. Hunter Lovins, *Brittle Power: Energy Strategy for National Security* (Boston: Brick House, 1982).

Social defence and the environment 101

Another option is to accomplish the things done by large-scale industry in a different way. The things done using the electrical output of large fossil fuel, hydroelectric or nuclear power plants can be done instead by a range of small local measures including insulation, solar design, solar hot water, wind power and others. There is not a direct need for every bit of electricity that is produced, since some is used to heat water or air.

A third option for replacing large-scale industry is to no longer consume the thing that was produced. This applies most obviously to planned obsolescence: throwaway containers and products that quickly break down or go out of fashion.

Of these three options for replacing large-scale industry, the latter two lead to a greatly reduced environmental impact. The first option, namely producing the same outputs using local small-scale operations, could have either a larger or smaller environmental impact. Replacing a coal-fired electricity generating station with burning of coal in households will increase local air pollution and perhaps greenhouse emissions. Steel minimills reduce transport costs for some inputs, but depend on electricity and may not be as energy efficient as an integrated plant.

So, local small-scale production does not *necessarily* lead to reduced environmental impacts, but this is certainly a possibility if the options of doing things a different way or consuming less are taken up.

Goods. To make a society resilient against attack, the goods produced should be designed to be durable, easily repaired and, where relevant, used again or for other purposes. This applies to clothing, building materials, consumer appliances, vehicles, communications equipment and machinery. If new production is sabotaged by an aggressor, people will need to get by with what they have.

There are in the community quite a number of people who are highly skilled in repairing things. They would have plenty of ideas on how to design things for durability and easy repair.

Design for durability, easy repair and use for different purposes goes against the grain of much current production, which is aimed at increasing sales by getting people to scrap the old and buy the new. The net effect is both increased production and increased environmental impact.

In the short term, a social defence system might require extra production to provide extra tools and goods for communities in case factories were shut down or imports cut off. But in the longer term, with an emphasis on production for durability and easy repair, the environmental impact would be considerably reduced.

Transport. A community's dependence on the automobile is a great vulnerability. There are several groups that can cut off petrol supplies: foreign oil suppliers, oil companies, and workers. Most public transport is also vulnerable to disruption. Rail systems, for example, depend on electricity or diesel; alternatively, a bit of sabotage of the rails can put the system off line.

The most resilient transport system is one based on walking and bicycles, with cheap, simple motorised vehicles for transport of heavy goods. Such a transport system implies a drastic change in town planning. Instead of suburban sprawl, people would need to live close to work, shops and services.

It should be obvious that this prescription for a transport system resilient against aggression and disruption is also one which greatly reduces environmental impacts.

Defence. With entire conversion to social defence, there would be no military production, leading to a reduction in environmental impact. But some of the requirements for social defence would have environmental consequences, as mentioned above: stockpiles of materials and energy supplies, decentralised production (which sometimes would use more materials than centralised manufacture), durable goods (which demand more materials in production, at least in the short term).

Social defence does not mean no defence spending: it means spending for different things.

Population. The size of a community has no obvious connection with the strength of a social defence system. The keys to nonviolent resistance are things such as morale, unity, the willingness to struggle and the capacity to struggle. A large population can succumb to aggression if it is divided and unprepared. A small population can mount an effective nonviolent defence, especially by establishing links with other groups around the world.

Therefore, social defence considerations don't lead to any particular stance in the debates over population size. Needless to say, a population on the edge of survival due to food or fuel shortages is not in a good position to wage nonviolent struggle—or violent struggle for that matter. A healthy surplus of food and other necessities is an advantage. But this is possible with a large or small population.

Wilderness. One of the standard dilemmas for social defence is how to defend unpopulated areas. The best answer I know is social offence: inform the world about the aggression, taking the struggle for legitimacy to the population from which the attack comes.

Whatever the answer to this question, it seems most unlikely that unpopulated areas are a special *advantage* to a social defence system. Hence, social defence gives no prescription for setting up wilderness areas, preserving virgin forests or protecting rare species.

This only goes to show that the changes needed for effective social defence are not identical to those arising from a radical environmental policy. It should not be surprising that there are differences; what is surprising is the number of similarities.

A capacity for social defence should not be treated as the paramount goal. If some changes for social defence lead to impacts on the environment, then these need to be weighed against each other. The outline of issues above suggests that conflicts in goals will be less frequent than compatibilities.

The question of monkeywrenching

Direct action against operations which threaten or harm ecosystems can be classified into two types. First is direct action carried out publicly, such as rallies and people chaining themselves to trees. Second is sabotage of tractors, billboards, survey stakes and so forth. This sabotage, commonly called monkeywrenching, is against property and is carried out covertly. As spelled out in the book *Ecodefense*,[3] harm to humans is to be avoided at all costs, both for moral and political reasons.

---

3 Dave Foreman and Bill Haywood (eds.), *Ecodefense: A Field Guide to Monkeywrenching* (Tucson, AZ: Ned Ludd Books, 1988, second edition).

One problem facing monkeywrenching is that sabotage is widely seen as morally reprehensible. In capitalist societies, especially the United States, property is considered sacred. Many people get more upset about violence against property than they do about violence against people. It is important to challenge the sacredness of property but those who do so often must sacrifice support.

A more fundamental problem with much monkeywrenching is that it is inherently negative. It is almost always against the actions of someone else. Protest and sabotage can be powerful tools, especially by small activist groups against powerful forces, but by themselves they don't lay the basis for a positive programme.

The provocative journal *Processed World*[4] has had a number of contributions favouring sabotage of computers, office equipment and so forth as a challenge against soul-destroying work. The trouble is that the line between principled attacks on oppressive technology and mindless vandalism is often a thin one for outside observers, and perhaps even for the saboteurs.

The commonalities between monkeywrenching and social defence should be clear. Preparation for social defence implies widespread learning of techniques of nonviolent action (potentially including sabotage) which are already used by monkeywrenchers. More fundamentally, building a self-reliant society would mean stopping many of the capital-intensive, energy-intensive and resource-intensive projects which are the target of monkeywrenching, and replacing them with green social and economic development. Finally, monkeywrenching and social defence would be organised similarly: in a decentralised and locally autonomous way.

Monkeywrenching and social defence potentially provide support for each other. The practice of monkeywrenching develops and exercises skills which would be valuable to a social defence system. Of special importance is the skill and sensitivity to carry out sabotage without any threat to human life.

Much of the nonviolent action undertaken in both the environmental and peace movements has been reactive: used against initiatives taken by developers and militaries. This is certainly the case for monkeywrenching, which is action *against* activities by industries and governments. By contrast, social defence includes

---

4 *Processed World*, 41 Sutter Street #1829, San Francisco CA 94104, USA.

Social defence and the environment 105

a positive programme for social reorganisation which involves mass participation using nonviolent action. As such, it has the most in common with positive programmes for the development of an environmentally sound society, such as the bioregional movement, that incorporate nonviolent action to promote and sustain them.

The infiltration of the US Earth First! movement by the FBI shows that monkeywrenchers need a wider analysis of power structures. It is simplistic to imagine that isolated individuals and groups can use covert actions against developers without a counter-attack. There is a degree of sympathy for monkeywrenchers because environmental perspectives have a large following in society—and this is due to the hard work of environmentalists, both mainstream and radical, in open, public campaigns.

Indeed, it is questionable whether covert violence against property is really such a powerful method of action. It lays the movement open to allegations of "terrorism," however false and misleading they may be. More importantly, the response of monkeywrenchers to government repression is to go even further underground. Dave Foreman, guru of Earth First!, recommends being even more secretive and careful. This is not the way to build a movement for social change. Instead, it encourages action without the benefit of dialogue and debate, and makes it easier to blame environmentalists for irresponsible actions, whether they are carried out by sincere monkeywrenchers or by government agents.

From the point of view of nonviolent struggle, there is much greater potential in public mobilisations like the Redwood Summer campaigns in California which brought together environmentalists and forest workers. The viciousness of the verbal and physical attacks on the leaders of these campaigns—most notably the May 1990 bomb attack on Judi Bari and Daryl Cherney, Earth First! activists committed to a totally open, explicitly nonviolent approach—shows the seriousness with which these efforts are taken by the forest industries and their supporters in government.

11
Science and technology for nonviolent struggle

It is often noted that one quarter to one half of scientists and engineers worldwide are engaged in military-related research and development. This includes work on nuclear weapons, ballistic missiles, biological toxins, the psychology of fighting groups, and technologies for crowd control, electronic surveillance and torture. Critics argue that these scientists should be working instead on nonmilitary projects in food production, health, transportation, education and a host of other topics.[1]

For scientists, the choice seems to be between research for war and research for something else unrelated to dealing with conflict. It is uncommon for those who oppose military research to be able, through their scientific investigations, to promote some alternative means for promoting security.

Many of the things done by scientists in the peace movement do not require scientific training: holding meetings, writing letters, lobbying, joining rallies. Many concerned scientists write articles and information sheets about technical topics such as nuclear and chemical weapons. Still, this seldom has much direct connection with their ongoing research. When scientists take a stand against weapons of mass destruction, their impact stems more from the symbolic value of being scientists than from laboratory research.

---

1 Seymour Melman, *The Demilitarized Society: Disarmament and Conversion* (Montreal: Harvest House, 1988).

One exception to this pattern was the boycott by many scientists of participation in work related to the Strategic Defence Initiative. But the idea of a boycott of star wars research was not accompanied by an equally well-defined idea of alternative research.

One of the reasons why it is difficult to replace "science for war" with "science for peace" is that most strategies for peace rely on strictly diplomatic or political measures which pay no special concern to science. Peace treaties, disarmament proposals, common security measures and world government rely largely on the talents of diplomats, negotiators, politicians and, sometimes, social scientists. There are a few cases, such as the Pugwash movement, in which scientists and engineers use their specialist skills to help develop arms control measures. But most natural scientists are left to sit at the sidelines and wait for the agreements.

Social defence, by contrast, is an alternative to war that has a significant potential role for scientists and technologists.[2] It is useful to consider a number of different areas.

Industry. Often one of the main aims of an aggressor is to take control of industry. Therefore it is important for managers and/or workers to be able to shut down production. This was certainly a goal of many resisters to the Nazis in occupied Europe, 1939-1945. But what if the aggressors torture the workers or their families to force them to keep production going? One solution is to design manufacturing systems to include vital components which, if destroyed, cannot easily be replaced. Spares could be kept in a safe place, such as another country. Torture would not help to replace the components, and would become pointless.

In some industries, a better strategy might be to decentralise production so that it would be difficult for an aggressor to "take control" easily. It might be desirable for small-scale operations to be able to be easily disabled but also to be easily re-enabled.

On the other hand, in some cases the aggressor may wish to destroy industrial facilities in order to subjugate the population. In such cases, it would be important to develop systems that are resistant to sabotage by outsiders.

---

2 Johan Galtung, *Peace, War and Defense: Essays in Peace Research, Volume Two* (Copenhagen: Christian Ejlers, 1976), pp. 378-426.

There are numerous industrial design problems requiring research and development. It should be clear that these problems cannot be addressed as isolated technical puzzles. The meshing of technical and social domains is crucial, and close consultation would need to be made with workers and others.

Food, energy, shelter, transport. Against a ruthless aggressor, pure and simple survival becomes important. Basic services need to be maintained. Since some aggressors have tried to starve a population into submission, it is important to be prepared.

Large-scale monocultures are vulnerable to disruption. A more resilient food system would include many local gardens and food-bearing trees. Relevant research here includes seed varieties robust to lack of fertilisers and pesticides, nutritious diets from wild natives, and methods for long-term storage of food. Much "groundwork" in this area has been carried out by the permaculture movement.

Centralised energy supplies, such as power plants, are highly vulnerable. Small-scale renewable energy systems are much more resilient. As well as continuation of current studies of such systems, there needs to be investigation of systems that could be maintained in the face of hostile action. Easily repairable systems would be highly desirable. Similar considerations apply to shelter and transport.

Health. Social defence is based on nonviolent action by the defenders, but there may still be violence by the aggressors. For example, in the intifada, many unarmed Palestinian resisters have been severely beaten or killed by Israeli troops. (Many proponents of social defence argue that nonviolence by one side *reduces* the likelihood or severity of violence by the other side.)

In such a situation, it becomes important for there to be medicines and medical techniques that can be easily administered by non-specialists. There need to be strategies to maintain health in the face of occupation, food shortages, curfews, harassment and other contingencies. As well as physical health, psychological well-being is crucial.

It is also useful to be able to determine whether torture has been used, and to authoritatively show this to a wide audience. Demonstrating the violence of the aggressor is an enormously powerful technique.

Communications. There are a host of important areas in computers and communications worthy of development for social defence: nonjammable broadcasting systems; cheap and easy-to-use short-wave radios; miniature video recorders; encrypted or hidden communications via computers, telephone and radio; ways of destroying or hiding computer information. Some relevant systems already exist but are not widely available or known. (See the next chapter for a fuller discussion.)

The psychology of aggressors and resisters also needs attention. Studies in the psychology of obedience and resistance need to aim at insights that can be readily learned and applied by citizens.

Conclusion

Social defence provides an alternative agenda for scientific research and technological development. So far, though, almost nothing has been done along these lines. The problem runs deep, since whole fields of science have arisen because of military spin-offs; these fields have little positive potential. Other fields, which would be highly useful for social defence, have never been developed because funding is not available.

A social defence research and development programme would be quite inexpensive compared to existing military R&D. Yet, while money has continued to flow for military-related research, there has been little money for science and technology for nonviolent resistance. At the beginning of the 1980s, the Netherlands government courageously initiated a social defence research programme, although funding for only one of the many planned projects was eventually provided.[3]

Governments are unlikely to initiate a major switch in research funding towards social defence. The most likely source of change is scientists and technologists themselves, who can pursue projects

---

3 Advisory Group on Research into Non-violent Conflict Resolution, *Research into Non-Violent Conflict Resolution and Social Defence: A Detailed Research Programme* (Amsterdam: Netherlands Universities' Joint Social Research Centre, 1986).

that aid the effectiveness of nonviolent struggle. Supporters can aid the process by contacting scientists, telling them about social defence, asking them what things they would be able to do, suggesting some projects and seeing what they think, asking them to suggest other scientists to talk to, and getting their help in searching scientific and technological publications.

In the longer term, an orientation to social defence rather than military defence implies dramatic changes to science and technology. There would be, inevitably, major changes in priorities for research and development, because the likely applications would be quite different. In order for this to happen, the present influence over priorities by governments, corporations, militaries and scientific elites would need to be replaced by a much greater influence by a range of individuals and community groups. There would also need to be a change in the actual activity of research and development, loosening the monopoly by career professionals and allowing greater participation by those who are currently "nonscientists."[4]

If defence is to become a matter for popular participation rather than for state elites and professional soldiers, then, in a similar fashion, science and technology for nonviolent struggle should become much more participatory in all senses: in the way priorities are set, the way resources are provided and the way the work is actually done.

---

4 Brian Martin, *The Bias of Science* (Canberra: Society for Social Responsibility in Science, 1979), part V.

12
Telecommunications for nonviolent struggle

by Schweik Action Wollongong*

Telecommunications can play a vital role in nonviolent resistance to aggression or repression. Yet there has been no systematic development of telecommunications research, policy or training for this purpose.

We interviewed a number of telecommunications experts to learn how the technologies could be used in nonviolent struggle. We report our general findings and list a series of recommendations for use and design of telecommunications. This pilot project reveals the radical implications of orienting telecommunications for nonviolent rather than violent struggle.

---

* This chapter is adapted from a paper by Schweik Action Wollongong. Those involved in the project were Sharon Callaghan, Terry Darling, Debra Keenahan, Alison Rawling, Lisa Schofield, Rosie Wells and myself. The group is named after the fictional character Schweik (or Svejk), a soldier who created havoc in the Austrian army during World War I by pretending to be extremely stupid. See Jaroslav Hasek, *The Good Soldier Svejk and His Fortunes in the World War*, translated by Cecil Parrott (Harmondsworth: Penguin, 1974).

Examples

Communications are absolutely crucial to nonviolent struggle against aggression and repression. The following cases illustrate some of the roles of telecommunications.

• Indonesian military forces invaded the former Portuguese colony of East Timor in 1975. Their occupation led to the deaths of perhaps a third of the population through killings and starvation. By cutting off communications to the outside world, outrage over this repression was minimised. The Australian government aided in this communications blockade by shutting down a short-wave transmitter in the Northern Territory.

In November 1991, a massacre of nonviolent protesters in Dili, the capital of East Timor, rekindled international concern over Indonesian occupation of East Timor. This killing attracted attention because of the presence of foreign observers and videotapes of the killings, illustrating the importance of communications in generating opposition to repression.

• In Spain there was an attempted military takeover in February 1981; rebels occupied parliament and held 300 parliamentarians hostage for 17 hours. King Juan Carlos appeared on television and denounced those responsible. This act was vital in undermining support for the uprising.

• In December 1981 there was a military coup in Poland, aimed at stifling the Solidarity workers movement. The coup was accompanied by severing of radio and telephone links with other countries for several days, until the takeover could be sustained.

• In 1989, Chinese troops massacred hundreds of pro-democracy protesters in Beijing. In the aftermath, the Chinese government tried to cut off telecommunications to other countries. But fax machines continued to operate, providing information to outsiders and enabling informed overseas protests. When the Chinese government publicised a telephone number for reporting of "dissident elements," this information was leaked overseas, and people from around the world jammed the number by making continual calls, preventing it from being used for its original purpose.

• The Soviet coup in 1991 failed, in part, due to lack of control over telecommunications. Yeltsin's supporters got out the basic message—refuse to cooperate with the coup leaders and defend the Russian parliament—using radio, faxes, computer networks and leaflets.

• The peace movement in former Yugoslavia makes excellent use of fax and computer networks. For example, a message may be faxed from an antiwar group in Sarajevo to Zagreb, where it is quickly translated into English and put on a computer bulletin board, thus getting information from Sarajevo to thousands of people in a matter of hours.[1]

Telecommunications also played a big role in resistance to the 1961 Algerian Generals' Revolt, the 1968 invasion of Czechoslovakia and the 1987 Fiji coups, as described in earlier chapters. These examples show the crucial importance of communications in nonviolent resistance to aggression and repression.

Killings of unarmed civilians can generate enormous outrage, both in local populations and around the world. By contrast, the killing of guerrilla fighters gains relatively little attention—violence against violence is seen as legitimate, even when the sides are unevenly matched. But killing or beating of civilians has to be publicised. If repression is carried out in secret, there is little impact. Communications and publicity are vital.

The project

Schweik Action Wollongong is a small voluntary group of people who work on projects relating to social defence. Various members of the group are also active in other social movements as well as holding down regular jobs. We keep in regular contact with like-minded individuals and groups throughout Australia and overseas.

Our project on telecommunications and social defence commenced in mid 1990. We interviewed a diverse range of people from the areas of satellite communications, computer engineering, ham radio, computer systems development and community radio. We started by interviewing people we knew and branched out as we asked the people interviewed who else we should be contacting. The interviews were usually conducted by two members of our group, one of whom took notes. The notes were written up and circu-

---

1 Information from Christine Schweitzer.

lated amongst members of the group. Care was taken to ensure the anonymity of the interviewees.

From our point of view, the interviews had a very useful twofold purpose. Not only were they a valuable and interesting source of information on telecommunications capabilities, but they also allowed us to talk to other people about social defence. In this way the interviews were a goal in themselves, namely raising the issue of social defence, as well as a method for gaining information about telecommunications for nonviolent struggle.

Main results

We describe some of our main findings according to the type of technology used.

The **telephone** system is a wonderful means for mobilising against repression. It is readily available to nearly everyone, requires very little knowledge or training to use, and can be used to contact virtually any part of the world. Most importantly, it is a network means for communication. Anyone can contact anyone and there is no central control or censorship over what people say on the phone.

There are two important limitations to the telephone. First, it can readily be tapped, and individuals usually don't know when this is happening. Tapping can do little to stop large-scale opposition, because there must ultimately be people who listen to tapped conversations. If there are enough people in the resistance, the regime can monitor only a small fraction of relevant calls. Tapping in this situation is effective mainly through its psychological intimidation of callers who think someone is listening to their conversations.

A simple way to get around tapping is to use public telephones or simply a friend's telephone. For answering of phones, some of the systems which forward a call to another number are useful: the location of the person answering the phone is not readily known to the caller (or someone listening in). Also worth considering, as preparation for emergency situations, are machines that change the pitch and vocal quality of a voice, and encryption technology (which puts the message into code).

The second limitation of the telephone system is that it can be cut off selectively or entirely. This can be used against the regime or the resistance, depending on loyalties of technicians on the inside. Generally, the resistance would be wise to keep the telephone system operating. For that matter, any modern industrial society depends on telephones for everyday functioning. So it is unlikely that the entire system would be cut off except for short times, such as the aftermath of a coup or massacre. Resisters should build links with technical workers to ensure that the chance of this is minimised.

Fax is an extension of the telephone system to printed documents. All the same considerations apply, except that documents received are often available to anyone who happens to be around. Faxes with security codes overcome this problem. (This is similar to the lack of security in telephone answering machines.) Fax machines are much less common than telephones and require a bit of training, but are basically easy to use. Using faxes is much better when lengthy or complex information needs to be sent out.

Computer networks are excellent for person-to-person communication, but can also be used to send messages to several addresses at once, or put material on a computer bulletin board for all to read. They have the same limitations as the telephone system, namely the potential for being monitored or cut off by a master user (the person who controls the system and knows all the passwords).

Unlike telephones, computers are not so easy to use and are available to only a small fraction of the population, being relatively expensive. Computers are becoming cheaper, more widely available and more user-friendly each year, and will undoubtedly play an increasing role in communication in crisis situations.

In the case of emergency, it would be advantageous to be able to run computer networks on a different basis. For example, the master user's power to shut down or monitor accounts could be terminated. Such a change could be programmed to occur, for example, whenever a specified number of users inserted a special command within a certain time interval. The methods of doing this, and their implications, remain to be studied.

Computers have the capacity to store vast quantities of information, and this leads to new considerations. Some databases—for example, containing information on social critics—would be sought by a regime. One possibility would be to have plans to hide, encrypt or destroy sensitive information in case of emergency.

Short-wave radio is another excellent network form of telecommunications. It can be used to talk person-to-person from different parts of the globe. Furthermore, it operates as a stand-alone system, so that the plug cannot be pulled from any central location.

Calls on short-wave can be overheard by others with suitable equipment; as in the case of telephone, the more people who are using the medium, the less the risk to any one. The location of short-wave transmitters can be pinpointed, but the transmission site can readily be moved. An ideal way to ensure continued international communications in a crisis would be to have a short-wave system in every home, plus many additional public systems for anyone's use.

A combination of short-wave transmission and computer data produces packet radio, in which packets of data are transmitted. These transmissions cannot be listened in on, though they could be deciphered with special equipment. Packet transmissions can be sent up to amateur radio satellites and broadcast down to receivers later, even halfway around the world. Combined with encryption, this provides a highly secure method for sending masses of data.

The main limitation of short-wave radio is the limited availability of the technology and knowledge of how to use it.

CB radio is similar to short-wave radio, except for a much more restricted range.

Television and **mainstream radio** are much less useful against a repressive regime. Indeed, they are prime targets for takeover. The main reason is that a few people control the content and the transmissions; everyone else consumes the message. In this situation, the loyalty of both technicians and broadcasters is crucial. If stations are taken over, perhaps the best counter move would be for technicians to cause faults hindering transmission. But this cannot be the basis for a programme of resistance, since immense pressures can be applied to recalcitrant staff, or new compliant staff brought in.

With some advance planning, a takeover could be delayed and hindered for at least days or weeks, if not resisted indefinitely. But often the threat is not immediately recognised by all workers, so it can be difficult to obtain agreement for such action.

Community radio stations, in which community groups control programme content and participate in making station policy, are much better placed to continue speaking out. Preparations for emergencies at such stations have the added advantage of making many groups aware of the necessity for action in a crisis.

In the longer term, it would be desirable to reduce dependence on the broadcast technologies of television and mainstream radio and to increase the use of network technologies such as telephone.

It is important to remember that other forms of communications are important besides telecommunications. This includes talking face-to-face, leaflets, bulletin boards, graffiti, posters and the ordinary post. Telecommunications can aid resistance to aggression and repression, but they are not essential.

It is also important to remember that technology is useless unless people are willing to act. In this sense, politics, not technology, is the key to resistance.

Recommendations

Even with the present state of technology and people's awareness, telecommunications can be an important part of nonviolent resistance to aggression and repression. But there are also ways to improve the effectiveness of telecommunications for this purpose. We list them here under five categories.

Realising present capabilities. Right now, people are quite capable of using existing telecommunications to oppose a repressive regime. People need to be made aware of their own capabilities.

If the mass media of television and mainstream radio, plus large-circulation newspapers, are taken over, there are still plenty of avenues for independent communication. The telephone system is the most obvious. People need to realise that only a small fraction of phones can be effectively monitored. Those who are at greatest risk of being monitored should realise the possibilities for using other phones.

Those who have access to computer networks should be made aware of the potential for communication. This includes people working for banks, universities and large companies. Similarly, short-wave operators should be made aware of the crucial importance of their technology.

Technicians in vital areas—such as television broadcasting or computer networks—need to be aware of how they can help maintain communications among those resisting repression.

Learning to use existing technology. Most people know how to use telephones. Many more can learn how to use fax machines and computer networks. Run a practice session with friends.

An even greater commitment is needed to learn to use short-wave radio or packet radio. It is important for these skills to be more widely shared in the community.

Preparation. Knowing how to use telecommunications is one thing; being prepared to use them in a crisis is another.

Having a procedure for telephoning people in an organisation or network is important. The system should work even when some people are not available or some telephone lines are interrupted.

Developing lists of fax numbers is another useful step. On a computer network, lists of important contacts could be kept ready for an emergency, and perhaps hidden in a coded group so that others cannot inspect the list.

Another important part of preparation is simulations. A group of people can run a drill, testing out their communication systems in the face of a few disrupters. In this way the strengths and weaknesses of different systems can be tested. Also, people can become accustomed to acting promptly and sensibly in a crisis situation.

Designing technology. Telecommunications systems should be designed to provide maximum use to a popular, nonviolent resistance, and minimum help to a repressive regime. This seems never to have been a consideration in system design before, so it is difficult to be precise about what is required.

Is it possible to design a telephone system so that a speaker is warned if another party is listening in on a call? Is it possible to design a telephone system in which every phone can become—at least in emergencies—as nontraceable as a public phone? Is it possible to design a telephone system so that user-specified encryption is standard? Or in which encryption is introduced across the system whenever a specified fraction of technicians (or users) signal that this is warranted?

Is it possible to design a computer network so that the master user's control over accounts is overridden when a certain fraction of users demand this within a specified period? Is it possible to design a computer system in which encryption or hiding of data bases is automatic when there is unauthorised entry?

There are many other such questions. Perhaps, too, these are not the appropriate questions. The most effective design of a telecommunications system to operate against a repressive regime will depend on practical tests which cannot all be specified in advance. It is certainly the case that there are a host of difficult and fascinating design problems.

It is important to remember that the design is not simply a technical issue, since the most effective design depends on an assessment of people's skills, commitment and behaviour in a crisis situation. Good design will discourage aggressors and encourage resisters. In this context, being seen to be effective is part of what makes a system effective in practice.

Organising society. Telecommunications is only one part of nonviolent resistance to aggression. Other areas are important too, such as energy, agriculture and industry, as described in other chapters.

Whether the changes in the organisation of society involve production of goods or political decision-making, there are implications for communication. For example, if a regime tried to repress dissent by interrupting deliveries of food, then it would be vital to have reliable communication about available supplies, local gardens, needy people, etc.

All this would require preparation, organisation, commitment and training.

We found the telecommunications project stimulating and challenging. We learned a lot about telecommunications and also about interviewing. By working in a group, we learned from each other and provided support for keeping the work going.

The telecommunications project is just one of an enormous number of possible community research projects. Some other groups that could be approached are salespeople, clerical workers, factory workers, transport workers, school students, teachers, workers in the building trades (including plumbers, carpenters and electricians), actors, health workers, farmers, police and soldiers.

13
Towards a resilient political system

Suppose that a community aims to defend itself from outside aggression by using nonviolent methods. The first thing that an aggressor would think of doing is applying pressure to the leaders of the community, whether they are presidents, mayors, church figures, business executives or trade union officials.

It would be relatively easy to capture and torture these individuals, or even kill them. But, in some cases, this might only antagonise the rest of the population and make conquest more difficult.

Another strategy for the aggressor is to win the cooperation of the leaders. This could be by offering them bribes such as money or a powerful position, or by threats to them personally or their families and friends. In either case, if leaders cooperated with the aggressor, this might well confuse and demoralise the population and make resistance more difficult.

For these reasons, any social system with powerful or charismatic figures at the top is vulnerable to takeover. The more powerful the figures, the greater the vulnerability. This also applies to threats from within, and explains why military coups are most common in military regimes.

This vulnerability may be reduced—not eliminated—when leaders are as totally committed to the resistance as everyone else, and play a genuine leadership role. In most existing societies, though, leaders are unaware of the capacity for nonviolent struggle, because they experience politics as a process of negotiation at the top. One of the sources of failure of the 1968 Czechoslovak resistance is that most of the Czechoslovak leadership was unaware of the power of nonviolent action and made concessions to the Soviet government that undermined the resistance.[1] This suggests that grassroots activists must ensure that elites understand the dynamics of nonviolent action.

Another reason why hierarchical systems are vulnerable is that people at the bottom, the "nonleaders," have less scope for initiative. The more powerful and prestigious the leaders, the more likely it is that others will rely on them to act on their behalf. Therefore, the nonleaders do not develop the skills and experience in decision-making, strategy and action required to counter a sophisticated opponent.

A third reason why hierarchical social systems are vulnerable to aggression is that people are less likely to be committed to the system and less likely to be willing to defend it. I've often heard people—especially left-wing activists—say they wouldn't want to defend Australian society because it has a small rich elite while many live in poverty. There is no real democracy since a small ruling class manipulates politics to serve vested interests; human rights are trampled on; and minority groups suffer enormously from discrimination and harassment. If this is the view of some Australians in a country which is far from repressive by world standards, generating commitment is likely to be much harder elsewhere.

So, ironically, hierarchical systems are vulnerable at both the top and the bottom: those at the top may be coerced or coopted to serve the aggressors, while those at the bottom do not have the skills or commitment to defend the community.

Hierarchies come in various shapes and sizes: political elites and masses; economic inequality; male domination; racial oppression. All of them make a society more vulnerable to subjugation or internal takeover. The process can be summarised by the familiar phrase "divide and rule."

---

1 Jaroslav Sabata, "Invasion or own goal?" *East European Reporter*, vol. 3, no. 3, Autumn 1988, pp. 3-7.

For these reasons, promoters of social defence should be exploring alternatives to the standard hierarchical social systems.

Actually, it's pretty unlikely that social defence could be sustained in a society of the conventional modern kind, namely one with a central government, central law-making and central administration. The reason is simple. The government depends for its power ultimately on the military. Laws are enforced, if necessary, by the military. Government bureaucracies could be disobeyed if not for the coercion exercised on their behalf. In particular, taxation would be a precarious activity without the support of courts and police powers.

All this goes to the heart of the modern state, which sociologist Max Weber defined as a community based on a monopoly of "legitimate" violence within a territory. The state here refers to what is usually called the government, the legal and prison systems, the military itself, government bureaucracies and such operations as local government, state schools, welfare services and so forth. The whole thing would fall apart without the power to force acquiescence for the purposes of taxation and repression of challenges to dominant groups.

Nonhierarchical decision-making

To develop a stronger social defence system it is valuable to explore nonhierarchical social systems. Here I'll concentrate on the political system, namely the system for making collective decisions—the decisions that affect the entire community. A nonhierarchical political system means one without the state. This is a tall order, given the enormous power of states in the world today. The aim in discussing such alternatives is not to propose a sudden switch in which the state is abolished and immediately replaced by another system. Instead, the promotion of nonhierarchical political methods should be part of a process of transition to social defence, and vice versa.

Rather than propose a single model, here I note a number of possible directions, mentioning some of their advantages and disadvantages.

Smaller-sized units. Some of the greatest hierarchies and vulnerabilities are found in the societies with many tens of millions of people. Undoubtedly, the political and economic power of populous states—such as the United States, Russia, Japan, India, China, Germany, France, Britain, Brazil—is enormous, and so is their capacity for aggression. One way to reduce this problem is to promote smaller units.[2]

With a single unified society, an aggressor can target the key individuals and then have an entire administrative apparatus available for use. If instead, the same society were divided into 10 or 100 smaller independent, self-governing units, this central vulnerability would be removed.

The break-ups of Yugoslavia and the Soviet Union may provide greater opportunities for social defence. In Slovenia, for instance, there were strong initiatives to implement social defence on the withdrawal of Yugoslav national military forces. In the event, though, Slovenia set up its own military. The ruthless fighting in former Yugoslavia shows that, when it comes to war, small is not necessarily beautiful.

An even better model is the Swiss cantons, which are largely self-governing.[3] They also exhibit a remarkable degree of citizen participation in the defence forces which, however, are armed. But the Swiss system of popular militias has many more similarities with social defence than does the usual system of a national army. (Social defence has been called the nonviolent equivalent of guerrilla warfare.[4])

The obvious vulnerability of small units is that they are prey to large aggressors. But this handicap can be overcome with a network of mutual support and well-developed social offence.

Consensus. As a decision-making method, consensus refers to a fairly well-defined system of reaching unanimous or near-unanimous agreement by discussion, exploring disagreements and

---

2 The case is given by Leopold Kohr, *The Breakdown of Nations* (London: Routledge and Kegan Paul, 1957) and Kirkpatrick Sale, *Human Scale* (New York: Coward, McCann and Geoghegan, 1980).
3 This model is advocated by Frances Kendall and Leon Louw, *After Apartheid: The Solution for South Africa* (San Francisco: ICS Press, 1987).
4 Anders Boserup and Andrew Mack, *War Without Weapons: Nonviolence in National Defence* (London: Frances Pinter, 1974), chapter 4.

proposing alternative courses of action.[5] In a strict consensus procedure, just one person may be enough to stop a proposal for action and to force reconsideration. In a modified consensus procedure, a few people in a large group can block action. Consensus often leads to creative solutions because a majority cannot simply use its numbers to push through a decision. The strong objections of just a few must be listened to and treated seriously. The result is that when a decision is made, it has much greater support from the group.

Compare this to voting in a mass meeting, which can fall prey to demagogues, setting of agendas by those running the meeting, and disruption by vocal minorities. When a vote is taken, the losing side often has little commitment to the decision and may even leave the group.

Those who have been involved with consensus decision-making, whether in a group of 5 or 500, realise its strengths. But it has some limitations.[6] Most importantly, consensus breaks down with large groups where there are strong and fundamental differences in viewpoint. Consensus with a group of 100 is hard enough. With 10,000 it is frighteningly difficult to achieve near-universal agreement.

From the point of view of an aggressor, a group using consensus is difficult to take over. There are no formal leaders, and decisions can't be forced on the group so long as there is a resolute minority. Experience with consensus gives people greater strength in expressing and standing up for their views. This is ideal for resisting outside control.

On the other hand, infiltrators could easily subvert the consensus process by simply getting in a group and blocking agreement.

---

5 See for example Michel Avery, Brian Auvine, Barbara Streibel and Lonnie Weiss, *Building United Judgment: A Handbook for Consensus Decision Making* (Madison: Center for Conflict Resolution, 1981).
6 Jane J. Mansbridge, *Beyond Adversary Democracy* (New York: Basic Books, 1980) is a sympathetic critique. See also Charles Landry, David Morley, Russell Southwood and Patrick Wright, *What a Way to Run a Railroad: An Analysis of Radical Failure* (London: Comedia, 1985); Howard Ryan, *Blocking Progress: Consensus Decision Making in the Anti-nuclear Movement* (Berkeley: Overthrow Cluster, Livermore Action Group, 1985).

Frustrating and time-consuming deadlocks happen often enough even when all participants are apparently well-intentioned. A few people intending to wreck the process would face few open obstacles.

The greatest strength of consensus methods is their capacity to win over opponents by incorporating them in the decision-making process. Whether this could work against "consensus saboteurs" is unknown.

Delegate systems. A traditional anarchist model of society is a federation of self-managing groups. Each group, whether at the workplace, local community or whatever, would determine its own affairs and views in a participatory fashion. (The exact details of this "participatory fashion" are not tightly specified: it could be consensus methods or voting in a general meeting, for example.) That part is straightforward. The self-managing group can take care of itself.

Delegates are used for decision-making at a broader scale, involving larger numbers of people. A number of self-managing groups could join together in a federation. Each group would send one or more delegates to a decision-making body at the federation level. Delegates are supposed to be directly accountable to their group, representing its views rather than their personal views. Also, delegates can be withdrawn at any time that the group so decides. Decisions at the federation level would be advisory only, for consideration by member groups.

When dealing with very large numbers of people, a number of layers of delegates and federations would be required: federations of federations and delegates from delegate groups.

The power of this model is the autonomy of the self-managing groups and the skills and independence of the individuals in them fostered by the organisation of work and community life. Self-managing groups would be a nightmare for an aggressor, because many people, through their experiences in everyday life, would have the spirit, skills and solidarity to resist impositions.

But what about the delegate system itself? Although delegates are different from representatives elected from a large and anonymous electorate, nevertheless delegates represent a potential vulnerability in the face of a determined aggressor. Each group is likely to select delegates who are the most articulate, knowledgeable and ambitious members of their groups. Such individuals, after all, are the most likely to promote the group's interests. Once people become delegates, their skills, knowledge and personal networks are considerably increased, as they routinely interact with others at the heady level of collective decision-making. As a result, inequalities in political influence are likely to increase between delegates and non-delegates.

This means that top-level delegates—especially those many stages above the self-managing groups—become obvious targets for aggressors. They could be coerced or coopted, just like conventional political leaders. This then is a potential weakness of federation-delegate systems so far as social defence is concerned.

This problem can be seen, in a mild form, in the evolution of the German Green Party. At first the elected parliamentarians from the Greens were expected to behave like delegates, for example to step down and be replaced by another individual in a policy of rotation. But as the party remained in parliament, these original intentions were subverted. Talented members insisted on staying in office, with apparently good reason because their high profile meant greater public recognition and support for the party. The accompanying change has been a transition away from a delegate role to a traditional politician role, including alliances with other political parties and compromises on issues in order to be "politically effective."

Of course, the experiences of the German Greens are shaped by their immersion in a system of representative democracy which is fundamentally hostile to delegate functions, rotation and responsiveness to the grassroots. Nevertheless, the potential problem of delegates becoming de facto representatives, with accompanying weakness of autonomy at the grassroots level, is worth pondering.

Demarchy. "Demarchy" is the name given by philosopher John Burnheim to a political system based on random selection and functional groups.[7] Burnheim decided that the word "democracy" is

---

[7] John Burnheim, *Is Democracy Possible? The Alternative to Electoral Politics* (London: Polity Press, 1985).

so commonly associated with systems of elected representatives that he needed a different word for his model.

Burnheim started his analysis with a critique of the state and bureaucracy. He concluded that they must be abolished if there is to be truly participatory decision-making.

But he recognised that it's impossible for everyone to be involved in every decision. There simply isn't enough time for an individual to become knowledgeable about the details of education policy, transport, town planning, industrial policy, environmental issues and so forth. (Individual politicians can't do this either, even with the support they have from researchers.) So, in a large and complex society, what system can there be for all individuals to be involved in decisions about a myriad of issues?

The first part of Burnheim's solution is "functional groups." For each different "function" in a community, such as transport, education, health, industry and sport, there is to be a different decision-making group. In this model, a "community" is fairly small, perhaps on the order of tens of thousands of people, like a small town or a suburb in a city. Therefore, a decision-making group will be dealing with a local issue.

Remember that there is no government aside from these groups— that is, no state apparatus—and no bureaucracies to administer decisions. The groups *are* the government.

The other, second, part of Burnheim's solution is the method of choosing members for the functional groups: random selection from volunteers for a limited term on the group. Why random selection? Because it gives an equal chance to anyone who wants to be involved, and gives no special legitimation to the person chosen: they have not been selected by the people and have no personal or party mandate.

The combination of functional groups and random selection solves the classical problem of participation in a complex society. People can nominate for as many groups as they wish, and are likely to be selected at regular intervals since the size of the community is not large. Furthermore, they can still participate in "politics" in the community sense by expressing their views verbally or in print, lobbying, organising rallies and so forth. The decision-making groups are not remote politicians but members of the local community. Therefore, the potential for participation is great.

Because each decision-making group deals with a specific function, there is an opportunity for those selected to study the issues in depth. They can listen to the views of experts and partisans and can discuss the technical and ethical issues with each other. Therefore the problem of informed decision-making is dealt with by dividing decision-making into functions. By contrast, a system of electronic referenda, where every individual can vote on every issue, would maximise a superficial, uninformed participation.[8] A key to informed decision-making is dialogue and debate.

Both key features of demarchy operate to prevent the rise to power of ambitious individuals. Elected parliamentarians and executives are involved in making decisions on a wide range of issues, and thus have exceptional power. This does not apply to the groups in demarchy, which deal with functions. Secondly, with a system of random choice, an ambitious individual has no sure way of being selected. By the same token, the role of vested interests—industrial, professional, ideological—will be much less, because they cannot build up a system to patronise officials. Political parties become pointless, while lobbying becomes a difficult challenge when new faces appear at regular intervals. The limited term for membership in a group makes sense, since those selected have no mandate for office: they are there by the luck of the draw, just as in the case of a jury for a criminal case.

There are many other things that could be said about demarchy, such as the evidence from trial juries, the promising experiments in Germany and the US with randomly selected groups for decision-making on controversial issues,[9] the idea of "second-order groups" to deal with policy issues such as the specification, size and

---

8 F. Christopher Arterton, *Teledemocracy: Can Technology Protect Democracy?* (Newbury Park, CA: Sage, 1987).
9 P C. Dienel, *Die Planungszelle: Eine Alternative zur Establishment-Demokratie* (Opladen: Westdeutscher Verlag, 1978; second edition, 1988); Ned Crosby, Janet M. Kelly and Paul Schaefer, "Citizen panels: a new approach to citizen participation," *Public Administration Review*, vol. 46, March-April 1986, pp. 170-178; Ned Crosby, "The peace movement and new democratic processes," *Social Alternatives*, vol. 8, no. 4, January 1990, pp. 33-37.

relations between groups, links with workers' self-management,[10] and the unanswered questions about how decisions would be implemented. But I set these aside here, since my purpose is to comment on the implications for social defence.

The first and obvious point is that in a demarchy there would be no formal leaders of the community: no one who through formal office is in a position of overall authority. Therefore an aggressor would have a difficult time selecting out prominent individuals to coerce or coopt. Those who are currently members of groups have no special mandate; if they were arrested or killed, a replacement of equal legitimacy could readily be chosen—by random selection. (Only the brave need volunteer!) Nor is there any easy way to infiltrate the system, since the only legitimate way to become a member of a group is through random selection. (In consensus systems, by contrast, infiltrators can enter with no special hindrance.)

A second point is that demarchy encourages participation in the areas that are most crucial to its members, and this means that knowledge and skills are developed where they are most needed. If, for example, you have a special interest in education, you are likely to follow the debates, write letters, attend meetings, talk to members of the education group, and perhaps nominate to be a member of it. If you have no particular interest in fisheries policy or building design, you are likely to be happy to leave those issues to those who *are* interested—unless they seem to be doing something outrageous, in which case you may well decide to become involved. So, the more controversial the decisions, the more likely that those who are affected will join the debate. The upshot of this process is that, on any particular issue, there is likely to be either general agreement or informed debate. All of this implies an active political system in which there is active participation which is greater in the more controversial areas. The population is thus ideally prepared to resist aggressive impositions based on divisive appeals, such as ideology or ethnicity.

---

10 F. E. Emery, *Toward Real Democracy and Toward Real Democracy: Further Problems* (Toronto: Ontario Ministry of Labour, 1989); Merrelyn Emery (ed.), *Participative Design for Participative Democracy* (Canberra: Centre for Continuing Education, Australian National University, 1989).

Another relevant point should be mentioned here. One problem might be that certain categories of people—men, the well-educated, certain ethnic groups—nominate for groups more frequently than others. It is easy to overcome this simply by requiring that those chosen be statistically representative of the population in any way desired. For example, half the members of a group might be selected randomly from the women who nominate and half from the men. In systems of elections or bureaucracy, quotas are often considered unfair. They are perceived as a deviation from the alleged fairness of open competition. But random selection is not a competition, but a process for selecting people who are representative of the community. Statistical specifications are entirely appropriate.

There is a final and fundamental connection between demarchy and social defence. With demarchy there is no state and therefore no military. That means that there is no armed force to back up decisions that are made by the groups. The power of the groups therefore comes entirely from the legitimacy of the process of random selection, analogous to the greater legitimacy of a jury compared to a judge as being representative of community opinion.

Occasionally groups will make unpopular or even outrageous decisions. Those who don't like the decisions can simply refuse to cooperate. This is ideal training for nonviolent struggle.

Indeed, because demarchy has no state, it must rely on either social defence or partisan warfare (an armed citizenry). In either case, the structural vulnerability to outside aggression is minimal. What is there to choose between social defence and partisan warfare? A social defence system is less vulnerable to internal takeover since, without rigid controls, a system of arms production and training holds the seeds for repressive power.

Conclusion

Rather than just trying to introduce social defence into existing political systems, there needs to be a parallel effort to explore alternative political structures that can serve to make social defence stronger—and which are desirable in their own terms. Hierarchical systems are inherently vulnerable to takeover by aggressors, external or internal. Nonhierarchical systems are better. Smaller units, delegate-federation systems, consensus and demarchy each have their advantages and disadvantages. Each is worthy of further exploration.

A nonhierarchical political system is not a *prerequisite* for social defence. If it were, social defence would indeed be a remote dream. Neither is social defence a prerequisite for a nonhierarchical political system. Rather, it makes sense to develop initiatives and campaigns that move towards both these alternatives simultaneously.

Campaigns for nonhierarchical political alternatives can include a nonviolent defence policy, and campaigns for social defence can include methods for participatory decision-making. So far, efforts in both these areas are sufficiently small that they can get by with consensus in small groups. The challenge is to develop the alternatives to be able to handle mass participation. If social defence is ever to become a mass movement and a practical reality, it must include a method of decision-making that is compatible with it, namely a participatory method. Otherwise, it is likely to be subverted by the very forces it was intended to overcome.

14
Towards a resilient economic system

Current systems of economic production are implicated in militarism in various ways:
* arms production and the arms trade;
* regimented working conditions which mesh well with regimented life in the military;
* competition between states for economic superiority which is linked to military competition;
* economic exploitation (especially of Third World peoples) which is backed by military might.

The dominant economic system in the world can be called state-regulated monopoly capitalism. There is struggle for domination of markets by large private corporations, with strong intervention by governments. This general type of system has shown its compatibility with the warfare state, whether in the form of liberal democratic states, authoritarian states, fascist states or even socialist states (the latter called state capitalism by some). Is such an economic system the best basis for social defence?

Intuitively the answer must be "no." This becomes more obvious by listing a number of the basic structural features of state-regulated monopoly capitalism and seeing how resilient they are likely to be in the face of external aggressors or internal takeovers.
* Production of goods—especially production by the largest firms—is centralised in large facilities. An extensive distribution system is required.

- Labour skills are highly specialised.
- Competition is a key driving force. Firms compete for markets and profits. Individual capitalists compete for ownership of stocks, real estate, etc. Workers compete for jobs and high wages.
- The system is founded on the assumption of *scarcity*, namely that there is never enough for everyone. This applies even though the productive capacity of the system may be great enough to provide for all people's essential needs.
- There is enormous economic inequality. This is a consequence of the above features. Wealth and income are allocated to people according to their property and their jobs, which are unequally distributed. (An important mechanism of allocation is credentials, which permit only a minority to become lawyers, doctors, engineers, etc.) The result is dire poverty for some and immense wealth for others.

It doesn't take long to figure out that every one of these features makes a society more vulnerable to being taken over. Centralisation of production makes factories and facilities easier to capture or destroy. Labour specialisation makes it easier to control key areas, since workers with crucial skills can be made to cooperate through either threats or bribes. Competition and the scarcity principle divide the population and make it harder for people to cooperate against an aggressor. Finally, inequality also divides the population. A usurper, through a clever policy of carrots and sticks, can cause different groups to blame and confront each other. In essence, the usual capitalist economic system is vulnerable to a policy of divide and rule.

When examining the most frequently quoted cases of nonviolent struggle relevant to social defence—such as the Kapp Putsch, the Ruhr 1923, the Algerian Generals' Revolt and Czechoslovakia 1968—it seems that capitalists, whether small businesses or large corporations, seldom have played a leading role. Why not? Is it because they hope to continue their operations under any alternative regime?

The one great advantage of capitalism is the market, a system that works somewhat independently of state control. The market can provide many of people's needs—even if in a distorted, unequal fashion—in the face of a hostile takeover of the state. The so-called underground or black economy, namely a market between individuals that is hidden from state regulation, is the best example of this.

The limitation of the market, from the point of view of social defence, is its dependence on the state for survival. This may sound strange, considering the many passionate defenders of the market who decry government intervention. The reality is that government intervention is necessary to sustain the market. The question is not whether or not to have government regulation, but what sort of government regulation to have.

Without regulation, the capitalist market is highly unstable and inefficient. Governments act to provide education and training for future workers, build infrastructure such as roads and communications networks, regulate the money supply, stop the sale of dangerous products, and foster "structural adjustment" in stagnant industries. All this sounds pretty reasonable.

The market depends on the state in a more fundamental way, too. It protects the system of property and economic inequality. An owner may possess dozens of houses which are rented to the rich or even left vacant while others are homeless. The state—through its agents, the police—will protect the owner from any challenge to this property. Similarly, farms and factories are commonly owned by absentee capitalists, while the workers develop no equity in the enterprise through their years of labour. Copyright and patents are systems to protect ownership of information, once again protected by the state.

The system of private property is accepted by most people in day-to-day dealings. The police are readily called to catch thieves, even when the poor steal food from the rich. But occasionally there is a radical challenge to property, such as from a radical workers' struggle. In such cases the military may be called in to break a strike. In many countries, a military coup is the mechanism used against popular challenges to the privileged classes.

If capitalism is such a poor basis for social defence, what about socialism? If this means state socialism, namely Soviet-type societies, it is obvious that they exhibit even greater weaknesses. The state is more powerful and the entire society is more vulnerable to takeover. (Some would argue that these societies are already

Towards a resilient economic system 135

"taken over," and that social defence to defend state socialism is self-contradictory.) It is necessary to look in different directions.

Egalitarian economics

Let's begin with the general characteristics of an economic system that would effectively sustain a social defence effort. It's valuable here to think of radical changes from the present system. But the aim is not to dream up a utopia that becomes a prerequisite for social defence. Rather, specifying features of a radically different economic system provides a way of thinking about *directions* for initiatives now. Here are some prime features.

• Local provision of goods and services. This makes it hard for any group to exercise central control via the economy.

• Low dependence on highly specialised labour. This makes it hard for any group to exercise central control via coercion or cooption of a small group of skilled workers.

• Cooperation. People would share knowledge, skills, labour and goods to maximise economic well-being. With a cooperative economy, it becomes much harder for any group to divide and rule.

• Collective provision. This means that goods and services are provided to groups so that anyone can partake, rather than on the basis of provision to individuals according to their ability to pay. Public libraries, roads and public parks are examples of collective provision. This could be greatly expanded to areas such as telecommunications, equipment for building and agriculture, and even food. Collective provision reduces the possibilities for divide and rule, assuming that the control of the provision is local and decentralised.

• Rough equality. The principle of distribution should be "from each according to their ability, to each according to their needs." Ability or privilege or power should not be a basis for claiming greater material wealth. The incentive for participation in the economic system should be satisfaction and solidarity, not survival and status. In such an egalitarian economy, people are much more likely to work together against any threats.

To top off this list of features which are so contrary to the conventional capitalist economy, it is necessary to note that in this alternative system it would be a great liability to have a state.

136   Towards a resilient economic system

Why? Because the state exercises a centralised intervention into the economy. It would be a prime candidate for being taken over and used to exercise central control over the population. Because the state survives by extracting resources from the economy (most obviously through taxation), it must maintain surveillance over people and their transactions.

The power to tax and, just as importantly, to monitor people and organisations to be able to tax, is ideally placed for oppressive central control—precisely because it is a form of central control already. (Many would say it is inherently oppressive.) An economic system that is to be as resistant as possible to attack and takeover would be one without this apparatus for central control.

This system of local production, cooperation and equality sounds pretty utopian. Is it possible? There is not the space here to go through all the arguments, but it is worth mentioning a few.

Such a system is quite compatible with "human nature," if there is such a thing. All the evidence shows that people are quite capable of cooperation. In fact, if anything is "unnatural," it is competition.[1]

Related to this, there would not be any great difficulty in motivating people to work without competition and inequality. There is plenty of evidence that people work the hardest when tasks provide an inherent satisfaction and when what they do serves the welfare of others.

Who would do the dirty work? In a cooperative society, what is now considered "dirty work" would have less stigma. The problem could be removed by such work being equally respected or more highly rewarded or automated away.[2]

Finally, if some people didn't want to work, then so what? Today's economy is one of surplus production. Massive quantities of food and material goods are produced by a small fraction of the

---

1 Alfie Kohn, *No Contest: The Case against Competition* (Boston: Houghton Mifflin, 1986). For a critique of the psychological assumptions of conventional economics, see Mark A. Lutz and Kenneth Lux, *The Challenge of Humanistic Economics* (Menlo Park, CA: Benjamin-Cummings, 1979).
2 Vernon Richards (ed.), *Why Work? Arguments for the Leisure Society* (London: Freedom Press, 1983).

population, while many others are unemployed or sitting in high-paid time-wasting jobs.

The objection to an egalitarian economy on the basis of "human nature" is very similar to an objection to social defence, namely that people don't want to defend themselves. The military and the centrally regulated economy each depend on people leaving key functions to others. Defence is left to the professionals, the military and state security managers; the economy is left to corporate and government decision-making.

Of course, this turns things back to front. People aren't involved in defence because the military has monopolised the function. There are severe penalties against those who challenge the military monopoly. Similarly, people aren't involved in cooperative local production because it is marginalised or repressed. The government intervenes to tax, builds infrastructure to subsidise conventional businesses, and smashes attempts by workers to take control of production themselves.

The difficult question about an egalitarian economy is not psychology but mechanism. How is the decision-making about economic production and distribution to be carried out? We know the present system: a combination of the market and manipulation by government and large corporations. What is the alternative? What I'll do here is outline some of the mechanisms proposed for an egalitarian economy.

Markets. Some opponents of the state still believe in markets, but markets administered by communities rather than by governments. There are several models here.[3] One is to maintain a market in goods and services but get rid of the market in labour. The market would be used to allocate resources where they are most needed. Individuals would have work if they wanted it, but in any case would be guaranteed a satisfactory standard of living, largely through collective provision.

Another market model is a local money system, which would undermine centralised control. Yet another approach is barter. For example, under the LETS system, a record of "credits" produced and

---

3 For a principled position founded on no state, the market and nonviolence, see *The Voluntaryist* (PO Box 1275, Gramling SC 29348, USA).

consumed is maintained in a local register; this operates like an extension of baby-sitting networks in which parents build up or lose credits.

Then there is "universal capitalism," an undermining of capitalist inequality by making everyone an owner of capital.[4]

Cooperative arrangements. Economic activity, in this model, would proceed on the basis of voluntary agreements between one individual and another, or one group and another. For example, a furniture manufacturer needing inputs of timber would negotiate with timber producers to obtain suitable quantities or a person needing help in constructing a house would make arrangements with friends and neighbours .

But what is the mechanism of exchange? Well, that's what is difficult to grasp about cooperative arrangements: the economic system operates independently of exchange. People would work because it provides them with satisfaction and because it is expected of a person as a member of the community. (This is similar to parents, who care for their children even though they aren't paid for it.)

People would reap the benefits of the economy simply by being members of the community. But instead of a government providing a welfare payment to everyone, the provision of goods and services would be arranged by the community.

To say that the economy will work by "cooperative arrangements" is rather vague. There are some existing models on a limited scale, including cooperatives (in food, banking, crafts) and self-management at the shop-floor level. It is fair to say, nevertheless, that the operations of a cooperative economy at a large-scale remain to be worked out.

Gandhian economics. There is a well-developed literature on Gandhian economics.[5] The Gandhian model is built around local, village-level self-reliance. The following assumptions are involved:

---

4 Louis O. Kelso and Patricia Hetter, *Two-factor Theory: The Economics of Reality* (New York: Vintage, 1967).
5 Amritananda Das, *Foundations of Gandhian Economics* (Bombay: Allied Publishers, 1979).

- community self-reliance and mutual cooperation;
- bread labour (voluntary physical labour in the service of others);
- non-possession (no ownership of things not personally needed);
- trusteeship (goods and skills are used for the benefit of all);
- non-exploitation (reduction of privilege);
- equality.

Clearly, Gandhian economics is at fundamental variance with conventional capitalist economics.

Demarchy. It's possible to extend the concept of demarchy to economics.[6] For example, any development in a local area would have to be approved by a trustee body, whose members are selected randomly from volunteers. The trustees could take into account the goods and services produced, efficiency, environmental impact and compatibility with social values. (Needless to say, the decisions could be quite different from the usual priorities given to profit and managerial control.)

This idea of trustees is compatible with several models for the organisation of work. Those proposing developments could be either profit-making companies or self-managing groups.

Applied to land, this idea of trustees is similar to proposals by Henry George.[7] But the idea can also be applied more widely. Randomly selected groups could also be responsible for controlling the supply of money, systems of payment for work done and so forth. The details of such a system remain to be worked out.

Implications for social defence

Which of these models is most compatible with social defence? My preliminary answer is that they all look pretty good in this regard compared to state-regulated monopoly capitalism. Each of the models fosters local control, local skills and local solidarity. Most of them do without the state. As well, there are other possible alternatives with these characteristics.

---

6 John Burnheim, *Is Democracy Possible? The Alternative to Electoral Politics* (London: Polity Press, 1985), chapter 4.

7 See, for example, *Green Revolution* (School of Living, R.D.1 Box 185A, Cochranville PA 19330, USA).

140 Towards a resilient economic system

The real test will be the test of practice. Which models can actually work and provide a satisfying quality of life? Which of them will be undermined by competitiveness and new systems of privilege? Which of them can best resist attacks by groups favouring economic systems built on centralisation and inequality? Which of them provides goals that can be turned into effective campaigns today?[8] I don't think the evidence to answer such questions is yet available. In the meantime, moves towards egalitarian economies can only help increase the capacity for nonviolent resistance to central control.

---

8 Pierre Guillet de Monthoux, *Action and Existence: Anarchism for Business Administration* (Chichester: Wiley, 1983), in a delightful discourse, gives insightful comments about the economics of a transition to libertarian socialism.

15
Postscript: Power tends to corrupt, even social defence

While I was visiting Troy, New York in April 1991, there happened to be an amazing story in issue after issue of the local newspaper, *The Times Union*. The story was about the Martin Luther King Jr. Institute for Nonviolence, which had been set up by the state government and funded generously with millions of dollars. As the name of this institute would indicate, it was supposed to be studying and promoting nonviolent alternatives.

The story was triggered by a draft report by the Inspector General of the state of New York into the affairs of the institute. The report alleged that there was gross mismanagement and other improprieties in the institute. For example, senior managers were said to use institute funding for improper purposes such as staying in luxury hotels, flying their families to conferences, treating themselves and their families to gourmet meals and purchasing personal goods. Some officials were said to run their own businesses during work time. As well as financial mismanagement, the institute was said to have abysmal staff relations. Well-paid jobs were given to family members and friends without adequate qualifications; the atmosphere was one of "anger, mistrust and frustration"; and there were cases of sexual harassment.

It is not my intention to make a special example of the Martin Luther King Jr. Institute for Nonviolence which, no doubt, has accomplished some excellent things. I use this example as a warning. Being involved with nonviolence or some other excellent cause is no guarantee against abuses, power plays and corruption.

Virtually every cause presents itself as noble, and yet how seldom are the ideals achieved! Christianity is based on a creed of love, yet the Christian church has been responsible for numerous brutal wars, millions of deaths at the hand of the Inquisition, and crucial ideological support for countless murderous regimes. Socialism promised a world without exploitation but state socialist regimes instead oppressed the workers and murdered millions. And, of course, military systems are set up to "protect the peace" but are responsible for war and torture.

Is social defence going to be any different?

There is a conspiracy of silence surrounding abuses within "progressive" social movements, just as there is surrounding the seamy activities of other institutions. Yet a few stories leak out.

• The left-wing Democratic Workers Party, based in San Francisco, had the highest ideals, with progressive policies, multiracial membership, female leadership and dedicated activists. All this hid an autocratic centre, where top officials gave themselves privileges while exhorting the rank and file to work to the point of exhaustion. Critics within the party were ruthlessly attacked while policies were changed and contorted to reflect the whims of the leadership.[1] No doubt such experiences are common in parties operating under so-called "democratic centralism," but seldom is the inside story told.

• Environmental organisations are not exempt from the dangers of power. These include decision-making by a de facto elite, some of whom have ties with governments, creating positions for high-paid administrators and lobbyists at the expense of local campaigning, and the dismissal of activists.[2]

• The United Nations, an organisation with wonderful ideals, was corrupted from the very beginning by a secret agreement

---

[1] Peter Siegel, Nancy Strohl, Laura Ingram, David Roche and Jean Taylor, "Leninism as cult: the Democratic Workers Party," *Socialist Review*, no. 96, November-December 1987, pp. 59-85.
[2] See articles by Hazel Notion, Timothy Doyle and Lorna Salzman in *Philosophy and Social Action*, vol. 16, no. 3, July-September 1990.

between the Secretary-General, Trygve Lie, and the United States government, which enabled US spy agencies to vet applicants for UN jobs. The UN was packed with people picked by national governments rather than on the basis of merit. Top officials were given exorbitant salaries. Kurt Waldheim was supported for the post of Secretary-General although the major powers undoubtedly knew of his Nazi past, because he could be relied upon not to challenge national prerogatives.[3]

How can social defence end up any differently? Basically, the creation of a new organisation, a new bureaucracy, must be avoided. Here are some suggestions.

1. Ensure that social defence operations are decentralised, autonomous and locally controlled. There should be no central administration or coordinating body. (Think, if you were in the CIA or KGB, how you'd go about infiltrating, controlling, manipulating or disrupting a social defence organisation. The very easiest way would be infiltrating or corrupting the people at the centre of the organisation.) Coordination can be done on the basis of networking.

2. Run social defence organisations democratically, whether this is by consensus, demarchy or whatever. Don't set up a bureaucracy, with hierarchy, division of labour, formal procedures and so forth, in which some people have much more knowledge than others and some people give orders to others.

3. Build social defence practices into people's lives—into their thinking, personal relations, everyday behaviour and the physical infrastructure of local communities. Social defence should be something that seems natural to everyone, rather than something handled by a special professional organisation. Once it is seen as someone else's responsibility, the opportunities for misdirection and corruption dramatically increase.

If social defence is an organisation, it can readily be subordinated to the military, government and other vested interests, kept under control and turned into a caricature of itself. Even turning

---

3 Shirley Hazzard, *Countenance of Truth: The United Nations and the Waldheim Case* (New York: Viking, 1990).

social defence over to social defence professionals is a prescription for misuse.[4] The solution is to make social defence part of people's daily lives.

Do you agree? Well, if so, how would you respond if a government or large corporation offered to generously fund a large number of positions to do action research on social defence in local communities? If you refuse, someone else, less scrupulous than you, will take up the offer. Certainly, it's an offer that is hard to refuse.

So, what do we do when the rich and powerful come to take over social defence? They haven't come yet, and may not for quite a long time. But it would be nice to have an answer if and when they do.

---

4 On professionals as a powerful interest group, see Charles Derber, William A. Schwartz and Yale Magrass, *Power in the Highest Degree: Professionals and the Rise of a New Mandarin Order* (New York: Oxford University Press, 1990).

Further reading

Here is a selection of English-language works dealing with social defence from a range of views. This list is introductory rather than comprehensive.

American Friends Service Committee, *In Place of War* (New York: Grossman, 1967).

Anders Boserup and Andrew Mack, *War Without Weapons: Non-violence in National Defence* (London: Frances Pinter, 1974). This is one of the more important treatments available. It is especially valuable in giving insights into strategy. In subsequent years both Boserup and Mack have promoted defensive military defence rather than social defence.

Bulletin of Peace Proposals, vol. 9, no. 4, 1978. A series of articles on social defence.

Civilian-Based Defense, 154 Auburn Street, Cambridge MA 02139-3969, USA. The key English-language periodical on social defence, with articles and news from around the world, including debates over directions for social defence.

Johan Galtung, *Peace, War and Defense. Essays in Peace Research, Volume Two* (Copenhagen: Christian Ejlers, 1976). Galtung provides some superb insights into the structure of society and the role of nonviolent alternatives. His writing is usually abstract rather than practically oriented, but is invariably stimulating.

Gustaaf Geeraerts (editor), *Possibilities of Civilian Defence in Western Europe* (Amsterdam: Swets and Zeitlinger, 1977). A useful collection of articles.

Steven Duncan Huxley, *Constitutionalist Insurgency in Finland: Finnish "Passive Resistance" against Russification as a Case of Nonmilitary Struggle in the European Resistance Tradition* (Helsinki: Finnish Historical Society, 1990). A provocative scholarly study investigating the complex social dynamics underlying a case often cited in literature on nonviolent struggle.

Gene Keyes, "Strategic non-violent defense: the construct of an option," *Journal of Strategic Studies*, vol. 4, no. 2, June 1981, pp. 125-151. Valuable history of the idea of nonviolent defence, and valuable insights from Denmark under the Nazis.

Gene Keyes, "Force without firepower: a doctrine of unarmed military service," *CoEvolution Quarterly*, no. 34, Summer 1982, pp. 4-25. Imaginative proposals for nonmilitary tasks for present military forces.

Stephen King-Hall, *Defence in the Nuclear Age* (London: Victor Gollancz, 1958). A pioneering effort, this book reads very differently from most others in the area, especially in its anticommunism and uncritical support for British parliamentary democracy. Nevertheless, there are some provocative suggestions for nonviolent defence, especially at the international level.

Brian Martin, *Uprooting War* (London: Freedom Press, 1984). Social defence is presented as a key feature of a grassroots strategy to challenge and replace the war system.

Adam Roberts (editor), *The Strategy of Civilian Defence: Nonviolent Resistance to Aggression* (London: Faber and Faber, 1967). An excellent collection. The essays that include criticism of social defence are especially useful for advocates.

Adam Roberts, "Civil resistance to military coups," *Journal of Peace Research*, vol. 12, no. 1, 1975, pp. 19-36. A highly useful survey with valuable case material.

Alex P. Schmid, in collaboration with Ellen Berends and Luuk Zonneveld, *Social Defence and Soviet Military Power: An Inquiry into the Relevance of an Alternative Defence Concept* (Leiden: Center for the Study of Social Conflict, State University of Leiden, 1985). A critique of social defence, using historical studies as well as careful analysis to argue that an invasion by a determined military power (specifically, the Soviet Union) could not be stopped by nonviolent means.

Gene Sharp, *Making Europe Unconquerable: The Potential of Civilian-based Deterrence and Defense* (Cambridge, Mass.: Ballinger, 1985).

Gene Sharp with the assistance of Bruce Jenkins, *Civilian-Based Defense: A Post-Military Weapons System* (Princeton: Princeton University Press, 1990). These books by Sharp are general arguments for civilian-based defence without much practical detail. Sharp remains steadfast in his advocacy of nonviolent action and social defence, and is indefatigable in his effective writing and speaking.

Index

Aas, Solveig, 90
abortion, 85-87
Advisory Group on Research into Nonviolent Conflict Resolution, 109
Afghanistan, 59, 67
agriculture, 96, 135
Albert, David H., 21
Algeria, 13-14
Algerian Generals' Revolt, 8, 13-14, 41, 113, 133
Algerian independence movement, 13-14
Alliance Party (Fiji), 51
Allies (World War II), 24-26
alternative: institutions, 7, 19, 22, 85; media, 57; research, 107
American Friends Service Committee, 145
American men, 44
American struggle for independence, 41
Amin, Amina, 83
Amnesty International, 57, 64, 68
anarchism, 77, 125-126. See also state, political system without
anarchist feminism, 82
Andrews, Frank M., 44
Angola, 67
antiabortionists, 86
anticommunism, 146
Aquino, Cory, 71
Arab states, 19
Argentina, 22
arguments: insufficiency of, 26; logical, 34; for social defence, 28
armed neutrality, 36
armed struggle, 13, 21, 81. See also guerrilla warfare
Armenians, 26

arms: production, 130, 132; races, 6; shipments to Fiji, 52; trade, 68, 90, 132
army, 5, 12, 35-36; officers, 16; rape and, 88. See also military
Arterton, F. Christopher, 128
attitudes to violence, 44
Australia, 10, 31, 52, 57, 59, 60, 61, 112, 113, 121
Australian Customs, 53
Australian Labor Party, 59
Austria, 31, 111
automobile, 102; industry, 97, 100
Auvine, Brian, 124
Avery, Michel, 124

Bain, Kenneth, 52
Bangladesh, 70
banks, 12, 18, 43, 55, 65, 117
bans by trade unions, 55, 60, 61, 62
Bari, Judi, 105
barter, 137
Bavandra, 58
BBC World Service, 58
beatings, 89; of prisoners, 93
Beijing, 112
Belgium, 15
Berends, Ellen, 146
Berlin, 11-13
bicycling, 98, 102
biological weapons, 97, 106
bioregionalism, 105
black economy, 133-134
Blumenthal, Monica D., 44
Boserup, Anders, 123, 145
Boulding, Kenneth, 9
Bower, Tom, 25
boycotts, 7, 15, 38, 62, 65, 68, 82, 83, 84, 107

148

Brazil, 123
bread labour, 139
Britain, 9, 24, 50, 58, 90, 123, 146
Bulletin of Peace Proposals, 145
bureaucracy, 75, 85, 122, 130; demarchy and, 127; state, 28, 29, 33; men in, 80; social defence, 143-144
Burma, 22
Burnheim, John, 126, 139
Burritt, Elihu, 8
Burrowes, Robert, 43-44
Bush, George, 66
business: closures, 20, 21; people, 18. *See also* capitalism

Callaghan, Sharon, 111
Cambodia, 26, 59, 67, 93
Canada, 9
cantons, 123
capitalism, 13, 33, 58, 75, 98, 104, 132-134, 139; as gender-neutral, 87; military and, 80; universal, 138
Carthage, 96
cassette tapes, 20
casualties, 23
CB radio, 116
censorship, 54-55
Central Intelligence Agency, 57-58, 143
centralisation, 108, 133, 140. *See also* decentralisation
Chelyabinst, 97
chemical: industry, 97-98, 99, 100; weapons, 97
Cherney, Daryl, 105
Chernobyl, 97
chiefs, 50, 51, 58
child abuse, 91
child care, 80
Chile, 22
China, 65, 112, 123; Revolution, 74
Chomsky, Noam, 25
Christianity, 142
Christiansen, Gordon, 9
CIA, 57-58, 143
citizens' initiative, 35-36
civilian-based defence, 5. *See* social defence
Civilian-Based Defense, 28, 145
civilian defence, 5. *See* social defence
civil servants, 12, 15. *See also* bureaucracy; state
coal, 100-101

code, 55, 114, 115. *See also* encryption
Cold War, 72
collective provision, 137
combat soldiers, 81-82, 88
Commonwealth, 57, 58
communications, 23, 31, 55, 62, 68, 76, 78, 102, 109; equipment, 101. *See also* telecommunications
communism, 16, 20
communist parties, 18
Communist Party of Australia, 57
community defence, 4
community organising, 36
community radio, 113, 117
competition, 133, 136
computer, 55, 65, 97, 104, 109; networks, 113, 115-116, 117-118; programmers, 87
conflict resolution, 36, 92
conscription, 38, 73; for social defence, 30; total resistance to, 36
consensus, 123-125, 131
consent theory of power, 8
Constitutionalist Insurgency in Finland, 38-40, 48
Constitutionalists, 39, 42, 45, 46, 48
consumerism, 98
contraception, 85-86
conversion: of police, 92; of soldiers, 16-17
Cooney, Robert, 40
cooperation, 120, 135, 136; economic system by, 138
Coover, Virginia, 92
corporations, 43, 65, 117, 132; crime in, 93; men in, 80. *See also* banks; capitalism
corruption, 93-94, 141-144
Costa Rica, 90
coups, 11-14, 18, 56, 112-113, 115, 120, 134; constitutional, 59; deterring, 63; Fiji, 50-63; rape and, 88; revolution vs, 74
courts, 82-83, 122
credentials, 133
credibility, Soviet, 18
crime, 92-95
Crosby, Ned, 128
cultural imperialism, 84-85
Currie, Elliott, 92
Czechoslovakia, 16-18, 27, 41, 70, 113, 121, 133; military, 17

Daly, Mary, 84
Darling, Terry, 111
Darvi, Andrea, 90
Das, Amritananda, 138
databases, 115-116
Deacon, Ellen, 92
death camps, 25-26
decentralisation, 73, 107, 143; monkey-wrenching and, 104; of production, 32. *See also* centralisation
decision-making, 32, 78, 122-131
defence, 5 *See also* military; social defence
Defence in the Nuclear Age, 9
defensive military defence, 36, 145
de Gaulle, Charles, 13
delegates, 125-126, 131
de Ligt, Bart, 9
demarchy, 126-131; economics and, 139
democracy, 18, 32, 33, 126-127; as gender-neutral, 87; reduced by the military, 6-7. *See also* participation
democratic centralism, 142
Democratic Workers Party, 142
de Monthoux, Pierre Guillet, 140
Denmark, 24, 69, 146
dependency relationship, 22
Derber, Charles, 144
design: industrial, 107-108; of telecommunications, 118-119
dictators, 20, 22, 25, 29
Dienel, P. C., 128
Diet, Finnish, 38, 45
Dili, East Timor, 112
diplomatic recognition, 68
diplomats, 55, 78, 107
Direct Action, 57-58
direct disarmament, 75, 78-79
disarmament, 75, 107; direct, 75, 78-79; negotiations, 70
divide and rule, 121, 133, 135
Doyle, Timothy, 142
draft cards, 44
drugs, 93; trade, 29
durability, 101-102

Earth First!, 105
Eastern bloc, 70
Eastern Europe, 29, 33, 71-72, 77
East Timor, 65, 67, 112
Ebert, Friedrich, 11
Ebert, Theodor, 1, 9
Ebert government, 11-13
Ecodefense, 103
economic system, 43, 73, 132-140; demarchy and, 139; egalitarian, 135-140; Gandhian, 138-139; military and, 97-98, 132-133; state and, 136
education, 2, 31-32, 85, 98, 106, 129, 134; peace, 36; in telecommunications, 115
egalitarian economics, 135-140
elections. *See* voting
electricity, 100-101, 102
electronic referenda, 128
Elhauge, Edward, 92
elite reform, 27, 28-31, 34, 36, 37, 41, 69-70, 79
elites, 18, 70; research and, 110; state, 32; trade union, 33
El Salvador, 18-19, 21, 67
Emery, F. E., 129
Emery, Merrelyn, 129
emigration, 52
encryption, 109, 114, 116, 118, 119. *See also* codes
Encyclopaedia Britannica, 39
enemy, 29, 30, 36, 90
energy, 108; efficiency, 100; military and, 97; social defence and, 100
engineers, 106-110; and direct disarmament, 79
English language, 113, 145
Enloe, Cynthia, 80
environment, social defence and, 99-105; war and, 96-98
environmental: movement, 10, 45, 77, 98-99, 142; weapons, 96
equality, 135, 139. *See also* inequality
equal opportunity, 81, 82
Esser, Charles, 92
ethical tourism, 61
Ethiopia, 67
ethnicity, 50-51, 53-54, 58, 62, 93, 129-130
Europe, 9, 10, 47, 48, 52, 72, 73, 107
Europeans, 47; in Fiji, 50
Evans, Peter B., 94
exchange. *See* market
experts, 34, 87. *See also* professionals

factories, 20, 23, 31-32, 133; shut down of, 102; women workers in, 84; workers in, 87
family, 81, 93

family wage, 80
farmers, 16, 18. See also agriculture; peasants
fascism, 25, 132. See also Nazis
fax, 112, 113, 115, 118
federations, 125-126, 131
Fein, Helen, 24
female emancipation and social defence, 84-85
female genital mutilation, 84-85
female soldiers, 81, 88
feminism, 77, 80-87; social defence and, 82-87
feudal Europe, 73
Fiji, 50-63, 65, 113; military, 63; trade unions, 60
Fiji Labour Party, 51, 52, 53, 58-59
Fiji Voice, 52
Finland, 38-40, 42-48
food, 23, 103, 106, 108, 119, 135
Foreman, Dave, 103, 105
forest, 45, 103; industry, 98, 99, 105; workers, 105
fossil fuels, 100-101
France, 13-14, 15-16, 77, 90, 123; military, 13-14; Revolution, 73-74, 77
fraternisation, 16-17
functional equivalent to military defence, 40-41
functional groups, 126-130

Galtung, Johan, 9, 23, 43, 70, 107, 145
Gandhi, 8-9, 44, 47, 70-71
Gandhian: economics, 138-139; paradigm, 42-43
Ganilau, Penaia, 54
gays, 2
Geeraerts, Gustaaf, 145
genetic engineering, 97
genital mutilation, 84-85
genocide, 24-26, 59, 71, 84, 93-94, 112
George, Henry, 139
German Greens, 10, 126
Germany, 9, 11-13, 15-16, 24-26, 90, 123; 128
Gilbert, Martin, 26
goods, 101-102
Goodspeed, D. J., 12
go-slows, 20, 21
government. See state
graffiti, 83, 117

grassroots initiative, 3, 27, 31-34, 36, 37, 42, 69-72; in economics, 135
Great Soviet Encyclopedia, 39
Green Party, German, 10, 126
green politics, 77, 99. See also environmental movement
Green Revolution, 139
Gregg, Richard, 9
Grenada, 67
Grindstone Island, 9
guardians, 6, 28
Guatemala, 19, 65
guerrilla warfare, 21, 81, 113; social defence and, 123
Gulf Peace Camp, 66
Gulf war, 66-68

harassment, 83, 89
Hasek, Jaroslav, 111
Haywood, Bill, 103
Hazzard, Shirley, 143
Head, Kendra B., 44
health, 2, 106, 108
heavy casualties, 23
Herman, Edward S., 25
Hetter, Patricia, 138
hierarchy, 121. See also egalitarian economics; nonhierarchical decision-making
Highleyman, Liz, 85
high school students, 18
historical: examples, 10-26, 27, 40, 69; interpretations, 39
Hitler, 24-25, 41. See also Nazis
Høivik, Tord, 90
Hoveyda, Fereydoun, 21
Hughan, Jessie Wallace, 9
human nature, 136-137
Hussein, Saddam, 29, 66-68
Huxley, Steven, 38-49, 146
hypocrisy, 66-68

ideas, 46-49, 53
ideology, 37, 129; of prisons, 94
immigration, 2
imperialism, cultural, 84-85
India, 8, 50, 70-71, 83, 123
Indochina war, 96, 99
Indo-Fijians, 50, 53
Indonesia, 67, 93, 112
industrial design, 107-108
industrial society and military, 97-98

152   Index

industry, 2, 29, 107-108; social defence and, 100-101; sugar, 52; women in, 81
inequality, 134, 140; economic, 133; military-environment connection and, 97-98. See also equality
infiltration, 124, 143
infrastructure, 134, 137, 143
Ingram, Laura, 142
Inquisition, 142
insurrection, nonviolent, 18-19
intellectuals, 35, 79. See also professionals
intelligence agencies. See spy agencies
international support, 23. See also social offence
intervention, nonviolent, 7, 65, 67, 84
interviews, 113-114
intifada, 91, 108
invasions, 14-18
Iran, 19-21, 67; Revolution, 8, 19-21, 74
Iraq, 21, 29, 66-68
Ireland, 93
Islamic Republic, 20-21
Israel, 19, 67, 81, 108. See also Palestine
Italy, 31, 90

James, William, 8
Japan, 123
Jelfs, Martin, 92
Jenkins, Bruce, 28, 147
Jews, 24-26
jiu-jitsu, 76
job rotation, 32
Johnson, Victoria, 86
Juan Carlos, 112
judge, 130
jury, 130
just cause, 42-45
justice, 94

Kahn, Herman, 23
Kahn, Robert L., 44
Kapp, Wolfgang, 11-12
Kapp Putsch, 11-13, 27, 41, 133
Keenahan, Debra, 111
Kelly, Janet M., 128
Kelso, Louis O., 138
Kendall, Frances, 123
Keyes, Gene, 23, 146
KGB, 143
Khmer Rouge, 93
Khomeini, Ayatollah, 20

King-Hall, Stephen, 9, 24, 25, 146
Kohn, Alfie, 136
Kohr, Leopold, 123
Kuper, Leo, 26
Kuwait, 66-68, 96

Labour Party (Fiji), 51, 52, 53, 58-59
Lal, Brij V., 50
Landry, Charles, 124
Lange, David, 60
Latin America, 19, 52
leaders, 46, 120-121
leaflets, 7, 18, 19, 83, 113, 117
legitimacy, 60; of random selection, 127, 130; of social control by nonviolent action, 91; of state, 94; violence having, 29, 74, 89, 122; of war, 94
lesbians, 2
LETS, 137
letters, 58, 61, 64, 83, 106
liberal feminism, 81
liberation struggles, 81. See also armed struggle; revolutionary social defence
libertarian socialism, 140. See also anarchism
Lie, Trygve, 143
Lithuania, 72
lobbying, 36, 58-60, 61, 79, 85, 106, 142
Louw, Leon, 123
Loving, Lisa, 85
Lovins, Amory B., 100
Lovins, Hunter L., 100
loyalty, 53, 116; of troops, 21. See also fraternisation
Lutheran, 47
Lutz, Mark A., 136
Lux, Kenneth, 136

Mack, Andrew, 123, 145
Magrass, Yale, 144
Making Europe Unconquerable, 28
male domination. See patriarchy
Mansbridge, Jane J., 124
manufacturing, 107-108. See also factories; industry
Mara, Kamisese 51, 54, 63
Marcos, Ferdinand, 71
market, 133-134, 137-138. See also capitalism
martial law, 20, 51
Martin, Brian, 8, 29, 110, 146

Martin Luther King Jr. Institute for Nonviolence, 141-142
Martínez, Maximiliano Hernández, 18-19
Marxist analysis, 58
masculinity and violence, 81. *See also* patriarchy
massacres, 76, 112. *See also* genocide
mass murder. *See* genocide
mass warfare, 72-74
master user, 115, 118
Mathiesen, Thomas, 94
McAllister, Pam, 82
media, 15, 17, 22, 47, 54-55, 57-58, 62, 64, 67, 98, 117. *See also* newspapers; radio; television
mediation, 36, 92
medical profession, 18, 85. *See also* health
medicines, 108
meetings, 38, 55, 58, 106
megalomania, 20
Melanesians, 50-51, 53-54
Melman, Seymour, 106
men, 80-88, 130; as soldiers, 73. *See also* patriarchy
Men Against Rape, 83
mercenaries, 73
mercy killing, 24
methods in social defence, 7, 23
Michalowski, Helen, 40
Mies, Maria, 84
militarisation of police, 89, 91
military, 1, 5, 33, 70, 72, 73, 75, 123, 137, 142, 143; capitalism and, 80; as criminal, 94; Czechoslovak, 17; defence, 6-7, 23, 30, 40, 91; demarchy and, 130; direct disarmament and, 79; economic system and, 97-98, 132-133; Fiji, 63; industrial society and, 97-98; licensed to use violence, 80; nonmilitary tasks for, 146; offence, 78; problems with defence, 6-7; regimes, 71, 120 (*see also* coups); repression, 6; research and development, 106-107, 109-110; resistance, 16; revolt, 18; social control and, 91; state and, 80, 122; support for killings, 26; women in, 80-81. *See also* coups
mistakes, 7, 23
misunderstandings, 7, 23
money, 134, 137, 139, 144

monkeywrenching, 103-105
monopoly capitalism. *See* capitalism
Moore, Christopher, 92
Morley, David, 124
Morocco, 67
Moscow, 17
Movement for a New Society, 10
Myrdal, Alva, 70

napalm, 96
National Federation Party (Fiji), 51
national: defence, 4, 30; liberation, 81; movement, 45
nationalism, 2, 62
Nazis, 7, 13, 18, 24-26, 46, 93, 107, 143, 146
negotiations: disarmament, 70; social defence, 70
Netherlands, 24, 31, 69, 109
networks, 114-117, 143. *See also* computer networks
newspapers, 22, 54, 55, 117
New Zealand, 57, 60, 61
NFP, 51
noncooperation, 7, 12, 13-14, 15, 16, 38
nonhierarchical decision-making, 122-131
non-possession, 139
nonscientists, 110
nonviolence, meaning of, 44
nonviolent action, 10, 38, 39, 42-49, 60; abortion dispute and, 86-87; concept of, 49, 53; in environmental and peace movements, 99; in Fiji, 52-63; against Iraq, 66; leaders and, 120-121; against male violence, 82-83; monkeywrenching and, 104; against rape, 83, 88; science and technology for, 106-110; social defence and, 5; spontaneous, 10; teachers of, 92; telecommunications for, 111-119; the term, 47-48; types of, 7
nonviolent defence, 5. *See* social defence
nonviolent intervention, 7, 65, 67, 84
nonviolent patrols, 92
nonviolent policing, 91-92, 94
nonviolent struggle. *See* nonviolent action
nonviolent vs unarmed, 91
North America, 10
Norway, 7, 9, 24
Notion, Hazel, 142

nuclear deterrence, 41
Nuclear-Free and Independent Pacific, 62
nuclear power, 10, 86, 97, 99, 101
Nuclear Resister, 86
nuclear scientists and engineers, 97
nuclear war, 41, 96, 97
nuclear warships, 59, 97
nuclear weapons, 67, 70, 74, 86, 98-99, 106
nuclear winter, 96

offence. *See* social offence
officer corps, 18. *See also* army; military
oil, 100, 102; industry, 97, 100; wells, Kuwaiti, 96
Olson, Theodore, 9
On Thermonuclear War, 23
Operation Rescue, 86
organisations, 64, 65, 78
Ostergaard, Geoffrey, 71
ostracism, 82
ownership of information, 134

pacifists, 36
packet radio, 116, 118
Palestine, 33, 46, 91, 108. *See also* Israel
Panama, 67
Parkman, Patricia, 19
participation, 7, 30, 33, 45-46, 49, 72-74, 77, 82, 110, 122-131; incentive for, 135
partisan warfare, 130. *See also* guerrilla warfare
passive resistance, 5, 39, 47-48
Pathak, Ila, 83
patriarchy, 33, 75, 80-88, 121; crime and, 94
peace brigades, 68
Peace Brigades International, 65
peace camps, 66, 68
peace education, 36. *See also* education
peace movement, 9-10, 34, 36, 66-68, 77, 90, 113; and environmental movement, 98-99; scientists in, 106
peasants, 73, 90. *See also* farmers
people power, 46; in Philippines, 71. *See also* nonviolent action
people's disarmament, 75, 78-79
permaculture, 108
person-to-person communication. *See* networks
petitions, 7, 18, 38, 64
Philippines, 33, 46, 64, 67, 71

physicians, 18, 85. *See also* health
planned obsolescence, 101
Plate, Thomas, 90
Poland, 46, 65, 71, 112
police, 18, 44, 89-94, 122, 134; abortion dispute and, 86; conversion of, 92; industrial society and, 98; licensed to use violence, 80. *See also* secret police
policing, 91-92
policy studies, 34
political parties, 10, 36, 126, 142
political police, 90. *See* spy agencies
political system, 120-131
politicians, 85, 107; male, 80
politics and technology, 117
population, 102-103
Portugal, 25, 112
positive programme, 19, 71, 104-105
poverty and crime, 93, 94
Prasad, Satendra, 52
press. *See* newspapers
prisoners, 95
prisons, 83, 90, 92-95, 122
pro-democracy movement, 112
Processed World, 104
professionals, 32, 72-74, 137, 144
property, 133-134; and sabotage, 103-104
prostitution, 84
protection rackets, 94
psychological health, 108
psychology, 106, 109, 114, 137; economics and, 136; of ruler, 22
publicity, 84, 113. *See also* media
public statements. *See* statements
public telephones, 114, 118
Pugwash, 107
purges, 26

Quakers, 9
quasi-nonviolence, 86
Queen, 58, 59
quotas, 130

Rabuka, Sitiveni, 50, 54, 55, 57, 62
race. *See* ethnicity
racism, 2, 121; and crime, 93, 94
radical feminism, 82
radio, 14, 17, 54-55, 78, 109, 112, 113, 116, 117; ham, 113, 116. *See also* short-wave radio
Radio Australia, 58
railway, 18, 102; workers, 15, 17

rainforest, 47. *See also* forest
rallies, 7, 15, 55, 58, 64, 68, 106
Randle, Michael, 71
random selection, 126-130
rape, 82-83, 88
Rawling, Alison, 111
Redwood Summer, 105
references, 145-147
referenda, 128
reform. *See* elite reform
refugees, 56, 65
rehabilitation, 92, 94
renewable energy, 100, 108
repairability, 101-102
representatives, 125-126. *See also* voting
repression, 6, 16, 22-26, 30
repressive governments, 18-26
reproductive rights, 85-87
research, 34-35, 36. *See also* science
resilience: of economic system, 132-140; of political system, 120-131
revolution, 13; American, 41; Chinese, 74; defined, 74; French, 73-74, 77; Iranian, 8, 19-21, 74; Russian, 74; social defence and, 69-79
revolutionary social defence, 69-79
Richards, Vernon, 136
rifle, 74, 82
Rigby, Andrew, 91
Rings, Werner, 46
riot, 21; control, 90
Roberts, Adam, 1, 9, 14, 16, 17, 146
Robertson, Robert T., 52
Robie, David, 52
Roche, David, 142
role-plays, 32
Romania, 72
Romans, 96
Roth, Julius A., 85
Rothfels, Hans, 24
RU-486, 85
Rueschemeyer, Dietrich, 94
Ruhr, 15-16, 133
Ruhrkampf, 15-16, 41
Russell, Bertrand, 8
Russia, 90, 113, 123; army, 8; Empire, 38, 40, 42-46, 48; Revolution, 74
Russification, 38
ruthlessness, 22
Ryan, Howard, 124

Sabata, Jaroslav, 121

sabotage, 15, 101, 103-105, 107, 116
Saddam Hussein, 66-68
Sale, Kirkpatrick, 123
Salzman, Lorna, 142
sanctions, 66
Sarajevo, 113
sarvodaya, 77
satellite communications, 113
satyagraha, 44
Saudi Arabia, 66
scarcity, 133
scenarios, 69-72, 77
Schaefer, Paul, 128
Schmid, Alex, 146
Schofield, Lisa, 111
schooling. *See* education
Schwartz, William A., 144
Schweik Action Wollongong, 111, 113-114
Schweitzer, Christine, 113
science, 106-110; priorities, 110; for war, 97. *See also* technology
scientists, 106-110; and direct disarmament, 79
Scott, Dick, 40
Secretary-General of UN, 143
secret police, 16, 19, 73, 90. *See also* spy agencies
self-management, 125-126
self-reliance, 32, 33, 88, 138; in energy, 100; monkeywrenching and, 104
severe repression, 16, 22-26
sex education, 85
sexual assault. *See* rape
Shah of Iran, 19-21
Sharp, Gene, 1, 7, 8, 9, 11, 28, 29, 33, 34, 35, 36-37, 42, 87, 147
shelter, 23, 108
shopkeepers, 15, 16, 52
short-wave radio, 55, 57, 62, 65, 109, 112, 116, 117-118
Shridharani, Krishnalal, 9
Siegel, Peter, 142
Simpson, Christopher, 25
simulations, 32, 118
size, small, 122-123, 131
Skocpol, Theda, 74, 94
Slack, Alison T., 84
slaves, 34, 47
Slovenia, 72, 123
small size, 122-123, 131
social control, 90, 91

156   Index

social defence: arguments, 28; assessment of, 25; bureaucracy, 143-144; conscription for, 30; corruption and, 141-144; definition of, 4-5; demarchy and, 129-130; economic system and, 132-140; energy and, 100; environment and, 99-105; environmental and peace movements and, 99; feminism and, 82-87; Fiji, case for in, 63; goods and, 101-102; guerrilla warfare and, 123; human nature and, 137; industry and, 100-101; inquiries, 69; methods of, 7, 23; as moral alternative, 9; negotiations, 70; nonviolent action and, 5; official interest in, 72; in one country, 76; as organising tool, 33; patriarchal, 87; policing and, 95; political system and, 120-131; population and, 102-103; as pragmatic alternative, 9; as process, 3; references, 145-147; revolutionary, 69-79; science and technology and, 107-110; small size and, 123; spending, 102; sponsored by elites (see elite reform); studies of, 9; as supplement, 30; wilderness and, 103
socialism, 29, 132, 134-135, 142; with a human face, 16; in one country, 76; prisons and, 94
Socialist Workers Party, 57
social justice, 92
social movements, 37, 77, 142
social offence, 5, 23, 54, 64-65, 76, 78, 103; and female emancipation, 84-85
solar: design, 100-101; hot water, 101; power, 97
soldiers, 14, 21, 73-74, 110; Czechoslovak, 17; female, 81, 88. See also army; military
Solidarity, 46, 112
South Africa, 8, 65
South Korea, 22
South Pacific, 58, 62
Southwood, Russell, 124
sovereignty, 78. See also state
Soviet Union, 16, 19, 29, 41, 97, 112, 121, 123, 134, 147; credibility of, 18
Spain, 25, 112
speaking out. See statements
specialisation, 72-74, 135; of labour skills, 133
species, 103
spontaneous nonviolent action, 10, 27

spy agencies, 25, 90, 93. See also CIA
Sri Lanka, 65
Stalin, 26
starvation, 108
star wars, 107
state, 1, 29, 32, 33, 45, 56, 139; abortion dispute and, 86; as criminal, 94; definition of, 122; demarchy and, 127, 130; egalitarian economics and, 135-136; vs government, 59; intervention against coups, 60; intervention into economy, 132-134; legitimate violence and, 89; military and, 80; political system without, 122-131; power, capture of, 81; system, 31, 72. See also bureaucracy
state capitalism, 132
statements, 7, 52, 64
state socialism, 29, 75, 134-135, 142; as gender neutral, 87
steel industry, 100-101
Sternstein, Wolfgang, 16
Stockholm International Peace Research Institute, 96
Strategic Defence Initiative, 107
Streibel, Barbara, 124
strikes, 7, 11, 13, 15, 17, 19, 20, 21, 52, 89, 99, 134
Strohl, Nancy, 142
structural violence, 43
students, 18
Stuttgart, 11
Summy, Ralph, 22
surveillance, 89-90, 106, 114, 136
survival, 108
Sweden, 38, 40, 69
Switzerland, 35, 123
Switzerland Without an Army, 35
symbolic: action, 7, 106; figures, 54
symbolism, 62

talking, 117
Tamanisau, Akosita, 52
tapping, 114
taxation, 73, 122, 136, 137
Taylor, Jean, 142
Taylor, Michael, 50
technical workers, 115, 116, 117, 118
technology, 74, 82, 106-110; of Indochina war, 96; politics and, 117; of repression, 90; for war, 97. See also media; telecommunications

Index   157

telecommunications, 111-119, 135
telephone, 65, 78, 109, 112, 114-115, 117-118
television, 17, 54, 112, 116, 117-118
terrorism, 105
Third Reich, 13, 24-26. *See also* Nazis
Third World, 61, 93, 98, 132
Thoreau, Henry David, 8
Tilly, Charles, 94
Timerman, Jacobo, 22
Times Union, 141
Tolstoy, Leo, 8
torture, 89, 90, 106, 107, 108, 120, 142
total resistance to military service, 36
tourism, 55, 56, 57, 60-61, 62, 65
trade union, 15, 60, 61, 62; action, 64; bans, 55, 60, 61-62; elites, 33
training. *See* education
transportation, 102, 106, 108
treaties, 107
Tribune, 57-58
trusteeship, 139
Tsar, 38, 40
Turkey, 26

unarmed police, 91
unarmed vs nonviolent, 91
underground economy, 133-134
underground newspapers, 17
unemployment, 137
union. *See* trade union
United Nations, 56, 57, 142-143
United States, 9, 10, 18, 19, 25, 29, 44, 57-58, 59, 74, 85, 90, 93, 98, 104, 123, 128, 143
universal capitalism, 138
university, 117; students, 18
uranium enrichment, 97

Versailles treaty, 15
video, 109, 112
Vietnam war, 96, 99
violence, 17; cultural acceptance of, 81; legitimate, 29, 74, 89, 122; masculinity and, 81; meaning of, 44; against Nazis, 25-26; against people, 104; of prison, 92; against property, 103-105; in resistance, 15; structural, 43
visitors, 55, 65, 78, 84
Voluntaryist, 137
von Lüttwitz, 11
voting, 35-36, 51, 98, 124, 128, 130

vulnerability, 120-121; of centralised systems, 108

Waldheim, Kurt, 143
walking, 98, 102
war, 6, 14, 28, 142; as criminal, 94; criminals, 25; environment and, 96-98; cover for genocide, 26; mass, 72-74; system, 33, 35
Warsaw Pact, 16, 70
Watson, Ian, 45
Weber, Max, 122
Weimar republic, 11-13
Weiss, Lonnie, 124
Wells, Rosie, 111
Western communist parties, 18
Western Europe, 98
Western governments, 21, 25, 29
Western intervention, 84-85
Western Sahara, 67
Western women, 84-85
Westing, Arthur H., 96
West Pakistan, 70
wilderness, 103
wind power, 100-101
Windsor, Philip, 17
women, 80-88, 130, 142; in industry, 81; in military, 80-82
women's movement, 31, 35. *See also* feminism; patriarchy
workers, 13, 45, 99, 137, cane, 52; competition by, 133; factory, 31-33; forest, 105; in industry, 107; petrol supplies and, 102; challenge to property, 134; railway, 15; technical, 115, 116, 117, 118; women, 84.
workers' control, 31
workers' councils, 32
workers' self-management, 129
work-to-rule, 99
world government, 107
World War I, 8, 11, 12, 15, 16, 111
World War II, 25-26, 41, 46, 81
Wright, Patrick, 124
Wright, Steve, 90

Yeltsin, 112
Yoder, John H., 88
Yugoslavia, 72, 113, 123

Zagreb, 113
Zonneveld, Luuk, 146

Still available from FREEDOM PRESS

Brian Martin
STRIP THE EXPERTS

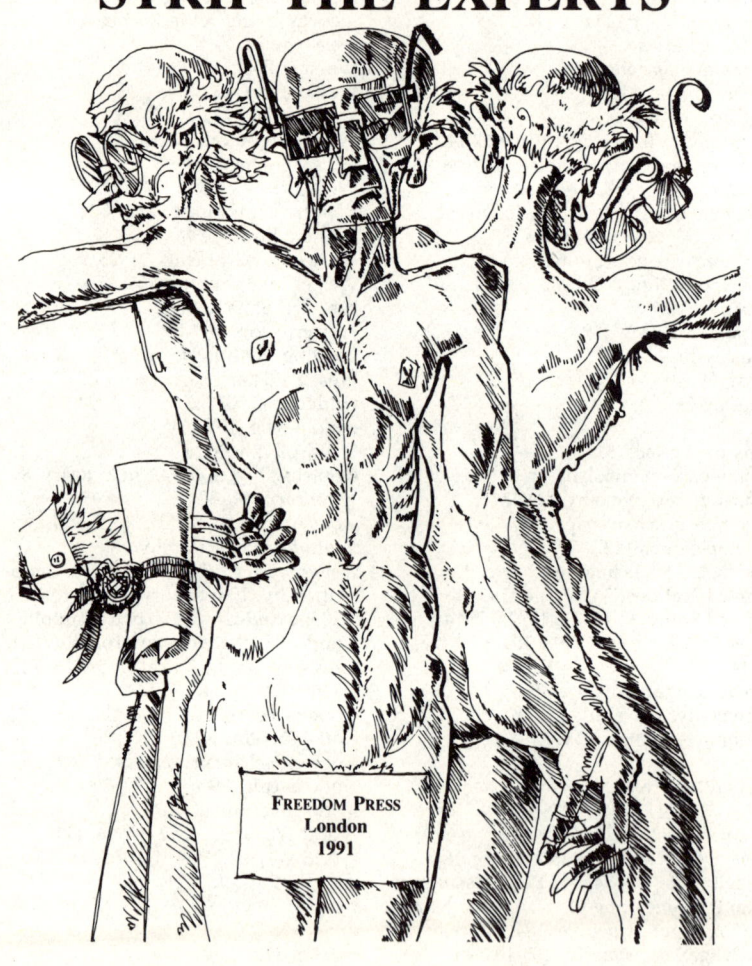

FREEDOM PRESS
London
1991

– two titles by *Brian Martin*

BRIAN MARTIN
Uprooting War

FREEDOM PRESS

A new title from FREEDOM PRESS

VIOLENCE AND ANARCHISM
A Polemic

Editorials and Readers' responses
from *Freedom* in 1960,
plus Appendices by Malatesta and Martyn Everett

"There is no greater error than to believe that we, as anarchists, need only to commit **any** deed, no matter **when**, **where** and against **whom**. To have a propaganda effect, every deed needs to be **popular**: it must meet with approval by an important part of the proletariat. If that is not the case, or if it actually meets with the **disapproval** of the very part of the population it is intended to inspire ... anarchism makes itself very unpopular and hated. Instead of winning new adherents, many will withdraw."

Johannes Most (1888)

80pp   ISBN 0 900384 70 0   £2.50